Sun...

Poems from Wild Places and Everyday Spaces

By Molly Remer, MSW, M.Div, D.Min
brigidsgrove.com

Sunlight on Cedar

Poems from Wild Spaces and Everyday Places

May you trust your magic. Love,

[signature]

By Molly Remer, MSW, M.Div, D.Min
ISBN: 9781676412915
Published by: Brigid's Grove
brigidsgrove.com

**For our patrons.
Thank you.**

And, for Mark Remer
who walks so steadily
through life with me.

Sunlight on cedar
crow on the wing
magic is real
it's in everything.

Note: a digital version of this book that
includes some additional short poems and
color photographs is available here:
http://www.brigidsgrove.com/sunlight-on-
cedar-digital-version-with-extras/

Table of Contents

Introduction

I am here
to marvel at
cathedralled branches
and the sounds of
newly birthed
water singing
to twilight.

June 2016

I am finishing my last semester of teaching at a college. I have four children ranging from 18 months to 12 years and a thriving home business. I am exhausted. I feel wrung out, weary, overloaded, sped up, and on the edge of collapse. My dominant fantasy, the one that pops unbidden to my mind as I work through my never-ending to-do list is just to lie on the floor, flat on my back. I tell my husband, "this isn't a sustainable pace for me. If I keep going like this, something bad is going to happen to me."

I keep going.

July 2016

I stand on the river bank with two friends and lift my arms to the sky. It begins to rain on us and I begin to cough. It is just a little cold, I decide. I continue teaching, working, mothering, going. I get a fever. I keep coughing. I cough through the last final exam of my college teaching career. I cough through Red Tent. I cough so hard through the month of July that I have to regularly sink down into a chair, out of breath, while trying to get going for the day. I try some "self-care" and finally grant my own wish to lie on the floor for a guided meditation. I cough so much that I cannot finish the meditation while lying down and have to sit up part way through. During this meditation (the "Moon Goddess Ally Journey" by Ros Simons), in the temple in which I meet the moon goddess, just as the meditation is coming to a close, the Cauldron rune from the oracle card system, *Womanrunes,* appears etched on the floor of the temple. The symbol is very large, covering the whole floor. It is dramatic and powerful and feels like a needed wake-up call. I decide that August will be a "Cauldron Month" for me. The Cauldron in *Womanrunes* is one of alchemy and change, but also of containment and contemplation—a marrying of what might seem like opposites, but that which really co-exist. During August, I vow, I will take it **all** to the Cauldron...to let it bubble and brew and stew and percolate. I will pull my energy inward to let myself listen and *be* and to see what wants to emerge. I give myself permission not to create for public consumption during this month, but simply to sit with myself and see what is bubbling, what is cooking, and how I might create a safe space for myself in which to stew up my truest magic.

While my time in the cauldron helps me clarify things, restores my sense of spirit, and gives me some time off to rest, I continue to cough. I cough through my children's birthdays and through the winter solstice. It isn't until I step out onto the beach in January of 2017, that my cough clears. In less than five days at the beach, the cough is completely gone.

(Why didn't I see a doctor for that cough? Well, because I am always pretty sure it will be better "tomorrow.")

June 2017

It is summer again. I have four kids who are all a year older and have more to do and more that they need from me. Our business is busier than ever. I feel tired. I feel wrung out, weary, overloaded, sped up, and like I'm burning out. I tell my husband, "remember when I got that cough last year? I feel the same way again, like if something doesn't give, I'm going to get sick."

My kids go to a social justice day camp and return with a hideous amalgamation of assorted viruses that concludes with revolting cases of viral pinkeye, eyes matted shut with yellow goop each morning.

July 2017

I hold out for many days, but as the last kid's goopy eyes clear, I go down hard. My fever recurs for weeks, one eye is bloodshot and streaming, and the nastiness settles into my sinuses where I develop a sinus infection. I go to the river, lie on my back, and fully immerse myself in the healing waters of the aptly named Cold Spring. I ask for my fever to be lifted by these cool waters. We go kayaking and look for rocks and watch a heron swoop overhead and little fish gather around our toes.

I realize I am angry with myself for being sick. I wasn't going to *do* this again this year, I complain. I'm only sick because I didn't *listen*, because I'm not taking good enough care of myself. I even google, "spiritual significance of sinus infection." Luckily, my gentler inner self takes my hand. She reminds me that I was the last woman standing in my family when it comes to this sickness, that I was actually the *strongest,* the one who waited until no one else needed me to care for them before getting sick myself. She speaks to me firmly when she says, "would you ever look your two year old in the goopy, disgusting eyes and tell him that he *deserves* to be sick? That he is only sick because he didn't take care of himself? If you wouldn't say that to a sick two year old, don't you *dare* say it to yourself. Ever."

August 2017

I honor another Cauldron Month for myself. Going on a solo vigil at the river. Journaling. Lying on the floor. Working with clay. Giving myself a break from working and content creation and generating work for public consumption. The sinus infection does clear, though in December I get another one which persists until I lift my arms to the sky by the ocean again in January. After only two days at the beach, the sinus infection is gone.

June 2018

Ah, this again. This sensation that my pace is not sustainable, that I need a break, that something has to give. I feel a tightness in my chest, a twinge in my nose, a constriction around my heart. I feel brittle and tired and strained. I tell my husband, "it is that time of year again. I'm doing something different this year. I am not going to get sick again." I ask my Red Tent to witness my promise to myself, that I am recognizing this as an annual pattern and I'm going to proactively head it off this time. I will be slowing down *now.* I will be saying no. I will be letting myself percolate, and bubble, and grow.

July 2018

I keep my promise to myself. I lay the groundwork for another Cauldron Month in August, scheduling posts in advance or deciding not to write them after all, deciding not to create new ritual kits or newsletter content, but rather to re-use the previous year's material. I let our customers know that custom orders are closed and that we are taking some time off. I shut off my personal social media accounts. I create new goddess sculptures. I sit on the rocks in the woods for an hour at a time instead of fifteen minutes. I write new poems. I try out radical ideas such as lying down when I feel tired. Stopping when I have a headache. Stepping outside when I need a break. Going to bed early and waking up with plenty of time for yoga and journaling. Saying no to things I could create and host and do. Not going to things. Stopping. Reading books I feel like reading. Sitting still with my hand on my heart and asking myself what I most need and then doing that. When I feel myself feeling tight and sped up, I do things like take off all my clothes and step out naked in the sunshine with my face lifted to the sky. I pick rose petals and hold them in my hand. I anoint my forehead with oil. I pick wild berries in the rain. I lie on the floor. We close our shop for an entire week and go to the river, where we sit in the water and go for walks, laugh together, celebrate our twentieth anniversary, watch the moon rise, and eat our favorite foods.

The Future

Listening to my heart, trusting my body, and taking care of myself is no longer a radical act that needs annual recognition and intensive planning. It is simply *my life*.

Pain and Pausing

"I pin my hopes to quiet processes and small circles, in which vital and transforming events take place."

—Rufus Jones

In the preceding section, I wrote about my own pattern of getting sick each July and the steps I have taken over the last three years to change that pattern for myself. In 2019, in a surprisingly literal twist, I fell and hurt my ankle in June, and at the time of this original writing, eight weeks later, I was still recovering from that fall, thus inadvertently continuing my pattern of spending July of every year "out of commission."

There is no dramatic story associated with my fall, I was quite literally just standing still on the front porch, waiting for my kids to open the front door after getting home from a Girl Scout meeting, when my foot slipped off the short front step and I came down hard on my ankle, twisting it beneath me at a 90 degree angle inward, as if I stepped down onto the end of my leg bone instead of my foot. I knew immediately that this was not a "normal" misstep or simple twist of the ankle, my leg hurt in a different and deeper way than I've ever experienced before, the swelling instantaneous and visible through my sock before I could even crawl inside. My husband Mark came running to help me and all I could say was, *I think I've really, really hurt myself.*

I have, in fact, really hurt myself. I tore ligaments in my ankle and fractured at least one small bone in the top of my foot. The bruises bloom immediately, deep purple and blue, along the entire edge of my foot, the top of my foot into two toes, and on my ankle itself, above the swollen, stiff lump where my normal ankle bone used to be.

My mom comes to bring me crutches, arnica tablets, and arnica gel and I tell her that I feel like I have *one day of this* in me and that's it.

Then, I cry.

I know that this isn't it.

In fact, I have much more than one day in me. I have eight weeks and counting.

When my dad who is a former EMT comes to look at my ankle, he accidentally makes me laugh by saying he thinks I will heal completely since I am "relatively young." I decide it is a parenting up-level to have reached a point in which you can accurately now describe your own daughter as *relatively* young.

As someone whose life is shaped by wings and walks, this is a hard circumstance to swallow. I feel like I have lost my joy, the twin bookends of delight that frame each day for me: my visits to the woods in the morning and my two to four mile walks each day with my husband. I usually move swiftly through my days, capable, certain, strong. It is strange to have gone from fully mobile and strong, to tender and vulnerable, in the space of only a single step. Of course, I wonder if this is a "sign," an enforced mandate to slow down and to rest, to be forced to take a break by being literally broken. But, then I remember the promise I made to myself two years before when I developed that nasty sinus infection after caring for my sick kids. If I would never look my sick toddler in the eye and asked him what he had done to "deserve" being so sick, I would never again visit that cruelty and needless blame-casting upon myself.

I see why animals who hurt their legs often die, I tell Mark.

I fall on a Tuesday and that Saturday, my mother comes to pick me up for our Red Tent retreat at the river. I am shocked by how unstable and unsteady I feel outside on the uneven terrain. I am barely capable of standing, let alone hoisting myself along the ground. I feel vulnerable and small, invalid and weak. My friend and my mom work setting up the simple ritual site and I watch, seated on the pavilion's porch, swinging my other leg and marveling at their adept and fluid movements, their bodily capacities, their sure feet on uncertain ground. The blankets are spread beneath swaying green trees on the point of land overlooking the confluence of two creeks and a river. We can hear the breeze and the gentle flow of the water. Women start to arrive, full of hugs and smiles and words of connection. I hobble to the blanket and sit down, where I can show my bruising and receive the tender balm of sympathy and exclamation. My chiropractor friend has traveled all the way from Kansas for our circle and she examines my ankle with care and a light touch, telling me though it may take six weeks, I *will* get better.

We gather in circle and I guide them briefly through shared breaths and grounding. A light breeze rolls around us, caressing our faces and our closed eyes as we rest our hands on one another's lower backs and hum together, surrounded by green trees, under a wide blue and white sky. A chorus of bugs and birdsong joins with our voices, the gentle drift of the never-ending river current hums, the ground is warm and whole beneath our feet. I have asked four of my friends to offer an elemental blessing with some herbs of the summer solstice and they circle us, speaking their carefully chosen words, scattering herbs to encircle our working. We sit and sing together, words of welcome and affirmation, love and wonder. Tears begin to fall from several women as the songs soak into our bones. I'm not sure what brings the tears, the circle, the song, the container, the sunshine on our shoulders. I look up to see four vultures cresting the bluffs and circling our circle with their own. We are here, we are alive, we are whole, we are well.

After passing the rattle and witnessing one another's journeys, we break for snacks and conversation and begin our projects: stamping designs on muslin tarot bags and doing batik dyeing. My mom drives me across the field to the river cabin to use the bathroom and I tell her I think I'm overdoing it. I feel frayed, ebbing, and weak. I know it is because I'm expending too much energy supporting the circle energetically, holding the space, the energy, the safety of our sacred container. She suggests I put my foot up and rest for a spell, and I do, letting the women bring me strawberries, chocolate, and crackers, and refilling my water, respecting my space, while they work on their projects without me.

After recharging with food and rest we move to our next item, an experimental, body-based concept I'm not sure will fly with our group, as it feels very intimate and personal. We divide into groups of four and take turns lying down on the blanket in the center of our smaller circles. The women around us gently lift up parts of our bodies and lay hands upon us offering the wish, the hope, the promise, the vow, the blessing: *let go.* While we occasionally laugh and some part of us initially feels silly, we quickly relax into the power of what we are experiencing together. This sun, this wind, this grass, these trees, this river, it all bears witness to the gentle care with which we treat each other. We touch each other so gently, so tenderly. It is surprisingly personal and intimate to be handled so kindly by our friends. I am surprised by the tender feelings I experience both when being the recipient of touch and in giving it to others. We are rarely so close to one another, leaning in, close to one another's eyebrows, toes, and weary shoulders. I place my hands on both sides of a friend's face and see the tears well up and spill over beneath her closed lashes. We re-gather in our larger circle, feeling connected and supported in a new way, and sing together two songs of letting go.

The other women go to the river now, for a ritual immersion and cleansing after our letting go. I can't accompany them, so I wait on my blanket alone, singing another song by Marie Summerwood: *let it in, let it go, round and round we flow, weaving the web of women.* I sing for a long time, high and quiet into the gentle air. As I sit alone above the riverbank, waiting and singing, listening to the hoots and laughter of my friends below me in the water, a red-shouldered hawk leaves the tree and glides away into the air where a vulture turns lazily above the river.

I am sad to miss out on everything I could be

noticing and experiencing with the rest of the group, but grateful for what I have seen.

The gift in this setback proves to be to recognize, as perspective often demonstrates, how much I *have*. I have spent any number of hours fretting over not getting to do something and feeling resentful of being impeded in my progress and now, thrown into a situation of *actually* being unable to do something and actually impeded, it brings into sharp relief the freedom and influence I truly enjoy the rest of the time. It feels much clearer to me now how often I don't do something for a multitude of reasons that are usually fully within my own control and choice, not because I "can't" or I am somehow not being "allowed to."

Movement is magical and I miss it, I think, sitting on the deck the next week in the cool air, watching the mulberry leaves and feeling the breeze bump against my heart. May I remember that watching and witnessing is one of my most precious and powerful gifts.

May I soften into limitation, relax my striving, ease my straining, and sink into resting.

My leg aches, but I am swept with gratitude for the new temple of the ordinary that I find has been formed by and on the weathered deck beneath my feet, and I am struck with gratitude that it is *only this*. Only my ankle. Only a normal, run of the mill fall. No lifelong trauma or catastrophic diagnosis. No permanent lifestyle change or disability, just a few weeks of hobbling and looking at the world from a deck instead of a rock.

A mockingbird flies onto the porch and lands on the windchimes. An orange butterfly opens its wings gently as it rests on the outer wall of the house. The lilies are full and gorgeous in the sun and a new red rose has opened on my rosebush by the deck.

I lie down on my back with my eyes closed and breathe.

Goddess of the sacred pause
please grant me the courage

to lay aside swiftness
and take up slowness,
to embrace limitations as learning,
silence as stabilizing,
waiting as worthy,
and sitting as divine.
Goddess of the sacred pause
help me to know stillness as strength,
patience as powerful,
and healing time
as holy necessity.

Postscript: it actually takes six months for my ankle to heal completely and it isn't until we go to the beach in January that I am able to once more pass the "hop test" (hopping on one leg on the injured side).

Winter

Do not deny yourself beauty.
You do not have to earn it.
I promise.
You are worthy as you are.

Solstice Moon

We watched three bats
dip and dive
over sun-streaked water
skimming so close
they left brief imprints
of their bodies on the surface
of the languid current.
We offered ourselves
a winter blessing
with cold spring water across
brows, throats, and shoulders
and heard a deer crunch
through fallen leaves.
We spoke aloud the
seed dreams
of cave time
and watched the
orange moon rise
over our promises.

New Year's Eve

And so the sun
sets on the year
in stripes of
pink and gold
and turquoise.
There is brilliant
green moss
beneath my feet,
gray clouds
drifting like smoke
from the North,
and golden bluestem
in the field
waving a gentle farewell.

Goals

I want to spy on the
red-shouldered hawk
that lives in our field
and learn about its life.

I want to discover more
secrets from the crows
who visit our compost pile
each morning.

I want to sit in the woods
on a rock every day
and listen to the birds.

I want to keep
a date with sunset
every night this year.

Leafshadow

What will I learn in the woods today?
There are deer to your right,
looking for breakfast.
They meet your eyes
in the stillness
and after a long moment decide
that you pose no threat
to continuing their morning walk.

The sun is shining on your eyelids.
making bubbles of light
dance in your eyelashes.
The moon is sinking through
the sky.

A hawk has taken flight from
a hollow tree.

Winter is singing to the sky,
through the skeleton of another
spring to come.

It is possible to make good friends
with a rock.

There are truths about living
written in the patterns of
leafshadow upon stone.

A Recipe of Wholeness

I am part wondering
and part knowing
part wandering
and part here.

I am part wishing
and part certainty
part wildness
and part still.

I am part watching
and part unseen
part wavering
and part firm.

I am woven of words
and wishes
these fragments
forming a recipe
of wholeness.

The Listening Hours

*Where might you find
a spot to nestle?
To watch and wonder.
To listen and feel.
To incubate your own being
and soothe your own heart.*

*This is cave time,
soul song,
heart call,
life beat.*

The listening hours.

Watched

This is a special place,
I told my three year old.
No, mom, he said
It is a magical place.

This morning I felt the
distinct sensation that
a deer was watching me
through the trees.
I half expected to come
face to face with it,
but instead I saw a squirrel
rustling through a cedar path
and birds alighting on oak tops
and decided I was mistaken.
I contemplated sunlight
and hackberries
and round yellow leaves on stone,
and watched birds playing tag
in the air.
I heard my son calling for me
so I ran up through the woods
and tapped on the window
to invite him to join me.

As I tapped,
I heard the snort and call
of a deer
near the porch
as it wheeled and ran off
through the woods
huffing and blowing as it leapt
over the stones.
It turns out
I was being watched
after all.

Underworld

I was pondering
the small mysteries
of shadowed spaces
and the mythopoetic storying
of our everyday lives
while kneeling at
the triangular opening
of a hollowing tree.
And, then the cat,
gave a curious nudge
and the goddess figurine
in my hand
tumbled away into
the darkness of decayed wood
I put my hand cautiously
all the way into the trunk
and reflected
isn't this how it is?
Feeling our way tentatively
into the Unknown,
reaching for Her
until our fingertips
make contact.

Beauty

Today woodsmoke
twined in tendrils
through sun-spangled cedar
as I coaxed coals back into life.
With the waxing moon hanging
in the blue sky
and cool air kissing my nose
I lifted my face to the branches
and whispered:
Beauty,
I am here to
see you.

Fire in Her Belly

She's got sunshine
in her belly,
mysteries
in her eyes,
waves in her blood,
and fire
in her hope.

She rises.

Centerpoint

Sometimes
at the ragged edges
of an unruly world
when life feels undone
there is a quiet
centerpoint
in which to dance
your
unbound
prayers.

Sunset at New Moon

Sunset at new moon
laid down a path
across the water
the twilight shadowed
sun sparkles
whispering
of a knowing
that requests patient
listening
and a wondering
that will kiss your dreams
tonight,
remembering
how in timeless
shadows,
you hear the yes
carried
by the waves.

The Seagull

We saw a seagull
with only one foot
upon the shore.
Set apart from the rest
by virtue of its otherness
it continued trying to join the whole
hopping gamely on one peg leg,
standing off-kilter in the surf
eyes on the ground.
We wondered what had happened
something fishing back, we said
but it flew and hopped and looked for snails
with admirable aplomb.
The end of the leg, while stopping at a point
was healed, not newly wounded.
We drew inspiration from this bird
telling each other
as we turned our shoulders
into the freezing wind
surely, we have as much gumption
as a one-legged seagull.
One night,
I dreamed I found its missing foot
among the seashells at the tide line

I held it in my hand
black, rubbery, forlorn
unable to return to
what it was.

Unchecked Wonder

We have walked together
at the moving edges
of the world
full of underwater mysteries
sun-stained magic
and unchecked wonder.

Lighthearted

Take a deep breath,
let your chest expand,
feel the tightness
near your heart
soften and ease.
Taste the freedom
in the air,
feel the singing
in your veins.

Wild Air

Breathing wild air
by the edge of the sea.
Freeing my heart
and allowing me to be.

Beach Song

It's okay to love what you love.
It's okay to feel what you feel.
It's okay to do what you do.
It's okay to be who you are.

(repeat until you believe it)

Devotion

There are things that ask
to be remembered
or, is it that I ask to remember?
The everyday enchantments
of our living,
words forming slices of
memory.
A white squirrel watching
from a sycamore tree,
the sounds of black
crows calling
from within the secret
passages
between oak tree
and neighborhood,
footprints of a shy orange
coastal fox in the sand.
Rays of sunlight
forming individual white rainbows
stretching from cloud
to water.
I no longer feel I have anything
to teach
I just want to tell you about the

shell I found today,
the sandy pink color
of its wave-shaped spiral
the way the pine needles
form a canopy under
which orange monarchs dance,
the surprising softness and bright
green hue of thin fingers of grass,
the pretty purple pollen cones
of a longleaf pine.
The colors of a morning woven
into a tapestry of devotion.

That is the word for this feeling
in my chest.
Devotion.
To noticing.

Gratitude

I am grateful
I am grateful
I am grateful.
May I remember
to have sunrise eyes
and open arms.

Art and Fire

You may ask if you
are worthy
if you have anything
of value to share
if your life has meaning
or purpose
and whether you have
work in this world
that matters.
Know that while you
stand on this spinning
world and wonder
there are wispy clouds
sending smoky wings of
twilight across a
deepening sky
creating a
unique and blazing
work of art.
Trust that you, too, are
a marvel of art and fire
and your wings are wise
and wide.

Earthsky Art

*One night I watched
the moon
turn red.
The next day
I watched the sky
become aflame.
This is the magic we
live in,
a living love song,
a moving prayer,
an ever-changing
tapestry
of earthsky art.*

Candlemas Morning

You are invited to
make space
for the enchantment
of your living,
the magical realism
of the world itself
right there in front of you.

Let your ears loosen
until you become aware
of the soundd of crows
conversing in three directions
underwoven by a low rolling
gobble from unseen turkeys.
A distant woodpecker adds
some staccato notes
that weave with surprising
delicacy over the branches
of winterworn trees.

From the mist rising
in the valley
cows low deep and insistent
and a rooster crows.

The sky is a patchwork
of puffy white and blue stripes.
The frosted purple canes
of raspberry arcing
from stone to stone
speak of June promises.

Let your shoulders drop
and soften,
let your fingers open
and spread,
and breathe in
the rising day.

New Moon Dreams

New moon dreams
hang in the air
as heavy and insistent
as the sky
which tolls
rain, rain, rain.
They ask
to be remembered,
but forgetting settles
in early
like the fog
while prismed droplets
rest easy
on mulberry twigs.

Two Worlds

Between two worlds
there is a quiet place
to sit
and the red-winged
blackbirds
alight softly
on cattails
over rain-soaked
earth.

Trust Yourself

You are vibrant
in this world.
Do not silence
the voice from within
or the singing of your soul.
Let the mist rising
from the forest
settle around your shoulders
like a cape
of possibility.
Let the colors of
morning grasses
delight you.
You know what you need
and you can trust yourself.

My Work

My work is to spin cells
into souls
into story.
To translate the mundane
into magic,
to tell the small stories
comprised
of gooseberry
and snowflake,
mushroom
and morning.
My work is to weave blood
and bones
into the holy,
to stand up for delight,
to listen for the whispers
of the wind,
and to tell of crowcall
and seedshadow.
My work is to remember
that it is my job
to take care of myself
and that only I can
hear the inner voice
that cries out

when I am starving
for myself.
My work is to be not enough
and too much
simultaneously
and to sit in the middle
of both
and just be okay
because that is all that I have.
My work is to ask myself over
and over
if anything really matters
and to still have the courage
to act as if it does.

My work is to keep opening
my eyes
my hands
and my heart.

My work is to watch
the sun shine
on that cedar branch
right now.

Delight

A full-bellied waxing moon
hangs watchfully in a gray-blue sky
while a heron of the same shade crosses
overhead
slow, silent wingbeats
coasting to the horizon.
The tips of the cedar branches are frosted
orange
with dimming sunlight
and I am enchanted by the way
the setting sun filters through
the bluestem grasses in the field.
I crouch down among them
finding myself suddenly transported
back to my childhood
sitting in a clump of the same grass
by the pond and feeling this same way.
Thirty years of time condensing
suddenly into
one seedfluff moment
of golden light.

Delight is waiting for you
to look for it.

Remembering Some Things

This morning I watched
a red-bellied woodpecker
yell at me from the top
of a sighing oak.
I spotted an armadillo
rooting through the leaves
in the labyrinth
and then scuttling away to
shelter beneath the porch
of my tiny temple building
where I surmise it has made
its home during winter days
that chill the blood.
The day passed and
I remembered some things:
You don't always have to
be inspirational.
It's okay to be tired sometimes.
Not everything is a lesson.
Sometimes life feels hard.
Sometimes life feels hard
because it IS hard
and not because
there's something

wrong with you.
Hugging each other
matters.
Then, I watched the sky
as it wove
a tapestry of amazing
color over the mud puddles
in the driveway.
And, that,
my friends,
is my news today

Gratitude Moment

Maybe it is time
to put a hand
on your heart.
To feel your breath
come in and out
and rest for a moment
in gratitude for this day
and for your own
powerful,
creative,
mysterious
beingness
on this earth.

Stopping

What if this was the year
you stopped?
Stopped
spinning,
forcing,
pushing,
scrambling,
rushing,
hurrying,
proving,
hurting yourself,
forgetting how to rest,
trying so hard,
expecting so much.

And, in the space
left behind
in the rich territory
uncovered
after all the straining
was set aside,
joy bloomed.

Backyard Journeys

I want to tell
small stories
about everyday
enchantment
and real magic.

I want to journey
in my own back yard.

Landscape

*I know how to write
the landscape of living
into language,
but the landscape of
loving feels too precious
and tender to attempt
to explain.*

For Mark Remer.

Tree Messages

Today we walked
along gravel
sodden
with snowmelt
where we spied
the branches
of a moss laden tree
extending like two antlers.
Another tree, with a split
in the trunk
formed an unapologetic
yoni of the forest.
The surprising purplish flare
of a turkey tail mushroom
spread from the base
of a tall dying oak.
As the sky dimmed into
stripes of pink and blue
cotton candy,
cleared cedar branches
flared into crackling sparks
of nightfall
and knowing
waiting for the full moon
to rise.

Light

*Sometimes the words
don't come,
but the light shines
anyway.*

Crossroads

Sometimes when
your world
looks askew
and you are parched
and flickering
you come
to a crossroads
of being.
There you discover
a place
to sit in the middle
of everything
with your hand
on your heart
feeling the thrum
of your conduit
to the holy.
The time has come
to tenderly
coax your own truth
out of hiding.

Catwalk

It was frosted moss
that first caught my eye
luring me down icy steps
and onto a patch of brilliant green
to delight in the tiny magic of the world.
Then, a black cat emerged
from the woods
to twine around my ankles
and meow insistently
as cats do,
when they're trying to convince
you to do something.
She would start off on the path
towards the woods
look over her shoulder
to see if I was following
and then return and meow
again when she saw I wasn't
listening properly.
After the push-pull of
three attempts
I followed her,
why not,
and stepped onto glassy stones.

As I breathed deep and came
home to my body,
I remembered a wise person said
if you don't have time to sit for ten minutes
sit for thirty.
I ended up having to crawl
off the ice-slick stones
onto the surer footing
offered by the crystalline moss,
but I returned home
satisfied in my skin again
and so was the cat.

Doorway

In the morning,
three deer leapt away
across the rocks
white tails waving
like flags.
Two crows arced overhead
following a well-traveled path
through the sky
above our roof.
The day proceeded
as days do:
food preparation,
straightening up,
talking,
asking questions,
settling disputes,
sharing ideas.
Full of motion
Need,
and action.
Evening fell
and we went for a walk
around the field.
In the upper corner

of the hill
by the woods
three deer again,
leaping away
white tails waving
like flags.
And, then a lone crow
tracing a solitary
and uncharacteristically quiet
line across the horizon.
These paired moments,
bookending a
chapter in the normal living
of a regular day
in a surprisingly graceful, tidy,
and enchanting way.
We see a thick cord of grapevine
forming an arch over a stone
a gateway to the Otherworld
or simply a doorway
into truly seeing this one.
We stand silently
by a green carpeted
boulder

one thousand
years in the making
appreciating reality.
This smallness and bigness
all gathered together
into one mossy
pinpoint of life.

Spring

Let the greening earth
glow beneath you,
let your buried power
rise and breathe,
for it is in being too awake
that you will know yourself
as whole and here.

Ostara Magic

Listen.
I sing the song of the spring:
a lover's kiss by firelight,
the blush of lilac
and violets,
the greening
and glowing
of the earth
as she breathes into
new life
and expands with joy.

Spring Muse

I listen to
fields carpeted with
violets
and swaying
branches heavy
with lilac bloom
and bees,
the whispers of spiderwort
and phlox telling
creekside secrets,
the sweep of heron
wings over blush-green trees
and the white moon rising
full-bellied
over a sunstreaked sky.
I know
the truth
of timeless renewal
and endless creation.
I rest in my own wisdom.
I inspire truth-telling
and heart-knowing.
I am nourished.
I am whole.

Lake Secrets

Two wild geese
are on the shore
beaks muddy
as they root through
saturated soil.
The passionate wind
has coaxed waves
into being
lapping at craggy
cypress roots forming
the banks
of this urban lake.
A bowl of roots
catches my fancy.
There is wildness here
I feel it
in the wind whipping
across my face
as I lean onto a cypress trunk,
rain splattering my cheeks
feet sinking into sodden ground.
Here, we are wild,
Secret,
unbound.

On the way back across
the parking lot
I hear the cry of a hawk
in the gray sky.
The lake and I now
share a secret:
what it feels like to
stand in the wind
and rain together
under a wide sky.

Tea. Time.

Today in the work room
I express a longing to add
another day to the week,
the world,
life.
It wouldn't take much
we laugh,
just an alteration
of time and space
and social convention
and a shift in
centuries old
agreements
and expectations.
Silence falls.
Then, one of us speaks:
meanwhile,
he says,
there is hot water for tea.

For Traci and John.

Spring Crone Knows

Listen.
I have watched
the lilacs bloom
for centuries.
Fields carpeted with
violets know
the truth
of timeless renewal
and endless creation,
each morning
a gift
to be greeted with delight.

I am cloaked in my own knowing
resting in my own wisdom.
I keep my own counsel.

I trust my heart
on this cyclical
journey of being,
knowing, and becoming.

Persephone Speaks

I have slumbered
in shadowed places
not knowing the surface
from the shore.
I have learned what it means to
rise soft-bellied from the deep
shards of darkness clinging
to my thighs,
my lips stained berry-red
with truth and desire,
my heart still capable
of shedding flowers
and drops of hope
on hungry plains
and stark forests
while mourning doves
rise from secret thickets,
and the yearning
in my bones
pulls me to both rise
and sink.
There is sunrise passion
in my eyes,
a pulse of longing in

my center,
a blush of firelight
streaked across my skin,
where sunshine
meets shadow
again
and again.

Blackbird Moon

Tonight a round moon
rose over a pale sycamore tree
dotted with birds
and alive with sound.
To the East, the metal
and concrete of the
skating rink,
the sound of trucks
on the highway.
To the West,
the sun setting
over an urban lake
beside a parking lot,
while red-winged blackbirds
chatted with one another
on the cattails
and I took a small moment
to breathe.

Essential Secrets

The wise pines
stand sentinel
over hidden
pools of dreams.
Step by step,
breath by breath,
stone by stone,
drop by drop.
These are the essential
secrets of the day.*

*"essential secrets" from Phil Cousineau's The Art of
Pilgrimage.

What If?

What if you can
dance with desire,
love with alacrity,
hope with fervency,
pray with your feet?
What if you can
open your arms to the sun
sit on cold stones
in the rain to watch for crows?
What if you can
step outside
and into being,
watch the sun rise
and set,
stoke your fiery core
of resolve within
to honor your own limits
to feel yourself as whole
and to know,
at last,
that you are unwilling
to hurt yourself
anymore.

Not a Problem to Be Solved

If life is not a problem,
to be solved,
but an experience to
be lived,
might you become aware
of the soft breath
in your belly,
the pull of awareness
in your back,
the dawning realization
that there is nothing to do
and nothing to prove
and you are safe
in being on this earth.
It is okay to be,
to watch,
to know and not know,
to be curious,
to soften into longing
and feel it spread
across your shoulders
and into the rise and fall
of your chest.
Where are you going?

Here.
What are you doing this for?
Love.
Do there have to be answers?
No.
What is the point of being?
Everything.
What if you are already whole?
Okay.
All right.
Right now.
Please.
We move through our days
anyway
because
and now.
In an ocean of not-knowing
there are undercurrents
of love and joy to
fuel your-my river of
being and becoming.
We're here.
Right now.

The Singing Night

Tonight we slipped
away into a luminous world
in which the ground
is carpeted with brown needles
and the sun is a red disk
sinking below boughs of pine,
while tiny landscapes
of mystical moss
nestle across slabs of stone.
A red-tailed hawk
swoops low over the hills
and the valley
is filled suddenly with
an energetic conversation
between barred owls.
We emerge from the trees in silence
feeling transported
and transformed
by witnessing
the birth of
this ensouled
and singing night.

Undoing the Knots

When it is safe
to say enough
I am satisfied
instead of fried,
heart-centered
instead of heart-sore,
content instead of coerced,
at ease instead of accelerated.

I am undoing my knots.

Rebuilding Your Soul

Expect to be enchanted.
Show up and pay attention.
Hold your wonder with tender fingers.
Be patient.
Watch for signs.
Take time.
Make time.
Feel it all.
Be more patient.
Wait.
Say yes to breathing easy
and to wandering.
Bleed if you need to.
Curl up.
Spread out.
Be still.
Move.
Wait some more.
Hope with your arms
wide open.
Expect magic to find you
and when she does
say yes,
I will,
and thank you.

Moonrapt

What if you bathed
in moonbeams
and they stained
your shoulders,
thighs,
and lips with magic
so that everywhere
you went
you would be known
as one who is
moonwise
moonwild
moonrapt
moonstained.*

**The word "moonstained" comes from Women Who Run with the Wolves, by Dr. Clarissa Pinkola Estes.

Too Awake

Be too awake.
Trust the trembling forest
place your hands on hot earth,
on cold stones,
in living streams.
Look for bridges into mystery
and thresholds into knowing
formed of leaning trees
and embracing roots.
Be too awake
and let wings of wonder
carry you into clouds of magic
winding wisps of pleasure
through your blood
and bones.
Be too awake
and drink
all kinds of moonlight
curling yourself into caves
and groves
alive with meaning.
Be too awake
for the world
is full of birds

and you can feel the singing
in your soles
and skin.
Be too awake
for there are lakes of longing
within you
and you know how to swim.
Let the greening earth
glow beneath you
let your buried power
rise and breathe,
for it is in being too awake
that you will know yourself
as whole and here.
Be too awake
even if it is the only thing
you have left to be.

Still Breathing

Today I made a choice
to leave behind the laundry
and follow sunbeams over
stones,
to listen to crows
and wander where they led,
to crouch on a carpet
of oak leaves and moss
listening,
listening
to hooves just a
few feet away.
I watched the sun set
through silent pines
and found a snail shell
in the grass.
A vulture circled my head
three times
close enough that I could
see its head turn
from side to side
and we both discovered
that I'm still breathing.

Recipe for Rebuilding a Soul

1 weary heart
2 open arms
1 large flat rock
As many tall pine trees
as you can find
1 empty book
Many pens
Lots of water
2 scoops of sunlight
An infinity of starshine

Mix together patiently and wait in the shadows. Let rise in the sun. Let rise with the moon. Check for delight. If still soggy and deflated, expose on a hillside or soak in the ocean. Sprinkle with laughter.

Submerge beneath a stream of inspiration.

Drizzle with dreams and a generous helping of time.

Steep with incredible slowness.

Dust with flowers and need well.

Let become exquisitely tender and soft.

When fully risen, warmed throughout, and glowing with strength and satisfaction, enjoy with a tall glass of moonlight, a side of magic, and a handful of enchantment.

Create regularly for best results.

Persephone Prayersong

Persephone,
please walk with me
through shadowed lands
with outstretched hands.
Across hills and vales
in unknown tales,
through dells
and dales
on misty trails.
Past sunny glades
and shady glens
straight up to
smoky, swirling dens.
Through foggy groves,
past quiet graves,
into the long
forgotten caves.
Through chambers of
the underworld,
through stories
that are rarely told.
Across plains of power
and pain-swept hours,
by singing brooks

and mossy nooks,
past shades of
what will never be,
by rivers stretching
to the sea.
Through valleys
of timeworn care
with steady steps
and honeyed hair.
With silent prayers
on red-stained lips
and flowers
on your fingertips,
with patient heart
and seeds of glee,
Persephone,
please walk with me.

Vulture Wisdom

I watched three vultures dance
over the Smoky Mountains
rising and falling,
dipping and weaving
in languid, leisurely,
lovely circles
buoyed by their own knowing
that they may glide
on the support
that surrounds them
as they appear and disappear
in turns into cool
gray-blue clouds.
We could learn a lot
from vultures:
Waste nothing.
Coast when you can.
Trust the support
beneath you.
Soar as high as possible.
Play with the wind.

Woodsrapt

We walk on a ridge of reality
between civilization
and wildness
in a land of
shadowed hollows
and mountain laurel
where cathedralled pines
form the only monuments
and great slabs of mountain
bones
stand sentinel over tiny cities
woven of root
and time.
We lose count of the crows
that guide the way to the
next secret
and the names of babies
etched on crumbling stones
tell of forgotten sorrows
and timeworn worries
in a valley of unknown stories.
I plunge my arms
into newborn waters
older than the hills

and let the current
wash away
my expectations
It is good to be alive
and breathing
in this woodsrapt
point of eternity
and change.

Message

Your Self is not an enemy.
You are not a problem
to be solved.
There is no shame
in knowing who you are.

The Mist

This morning
I heard the mist calling
from the forest
so I stepped along
a green pathway
pausing at a threshold
formed of hickory bough
and fallen oak
before entering temple silence.
On an altar of flat rock
beneath a gray bowl of sky
I was enveloped in a soft shroud
of presence,
watching trees that are
somehow both newborn
and timeless
spread their silent arms
and breathe.
I closed my eyes and
the sound of a lone wild goose
rose from the clouded valley
and crossed overhead
while a cacophony of crow voices
echoed on an unseen horizon.

Finally, I laid words aside
remembering that some things
are meant to be held tenderly
against the heart
unshared
and others drift away
on curls of mist
under umbrellaed leaves
and the curtain of time.

Careworn Soul

What do you do with a careworn soul?
Do you let the threads continue
to thin and unravel
until you drift away
on a gossamer breeze?
Do you accept the numbness
of heart
that threatens to freeze
your hope?
Do you let the tears slip
down the back of your throat
and choke on unsung dreams?
Do you coil yourself down low
until you become poised to strike
and barbs grow on your tongue
and fingertips?
Or, do you let yourself cry
until you find yourself
awakening to a new day
and the wild violets are in bloom?
Do you spin the fibers
of your remaining love
into a cord of courage?
Do you gather seeds of

almost forgotten dreams and nestle them
into the dark crevices that have formed
in your threadbare soul?
Do you find the cracks and holes
that have formed in your being
allow sunlight to peek around
the edges of yourself?
Do you let yourself become
soft and loamy
and feel the tender roots
of possibility winding down
into your bones
where you discover
something written on sinew
that feels like truth?

Hades

In a stolen moment
I followed
red-winged blackbirds
to the lake
where I knelt in wild
violets singing
and admiring a twisted tree
laden with pollen
and new leaves
rising from a knotted shore.
There are light raindrops
on my shoulders
and I look up to
discover I am
observed by a man
leaning on a cypress tree
He is not tall, dark,
and underworld,
but slight,
sandy-haired,
and young.
I feel self-conscious
and vulnerable
to have been singing

in the violets
thinking I was alone.
I speak to him anyway
and tell him I like
leaning on trees too.
He tells me about his run
and how this is his favorite place
where he comes to be in nature.
I leave him there
watching the ducks
part the green waters
and return from my sojourn
heartened to know
there are places of
peace in this world
that manage to speak
to disparate souls.

The Path of Magic

Keep putting yourself
in the path of magic.
Keep walking right up to
and into it.
Be willing to be
in the heart.

And:

If you are looking
for evidence
that the world is made
of magic
you will find it
everywhere.

Atlantis

I have guided
many through deep places
sometimes not knowing
the surface from the shore
yet still emerging
blinking in the bright sunlight
and holding the
richest treasure
I could uncover.
My Self.

On the Edge

There is courage to be found
in both rising and sinking,
love to be found in dark corners
and open spaces,
poems to be woven
of shells and bone,
hope to be twined
around crumbling hearts,
wings to be witnessed
unfurling
into
beyond.
I hold the quiet
I hold the storm
and I dance between them
on the rippling
edge
of the world.

Fortieth Birthday

Today I turned 40
and I gave myself the gift
of letting go
of the persistent shadow
of not being good enough.
It didn't want to let go at first
rooted deep
and twining through my brain,
but gradually it loosened
and lifted
until only one thin tendril remained
connected to the top of my skull.
I thought about
cord-cutting,
excision,
uprooting,
banishing,
but then I realized
I would do it no violence,
and would allow it to go gently.
I tried to let it soar away
on the wings of a crow.
I tried to let it flutter away
with a black and white butterfly,

but it wasn't ready to leave me.
I thanked it for how hard it
has always tried to keep me safe,
but still it floated above my head
all day
and it wasn't until I finally said:
I promise I will be okay
without you,
that it grew its own wings
and flew away into the gray sky
to coast with a vulture
above the trees
until they both dipped below
the horizon
and out of sight.

Kitchen Conversations

Our dinners are
frozen together.

> *Is that a poem?*

If we leave them sitting here
they might defrost
enough to separate.

> *Everything*
>> *is*
>>> *a poem.*

I don't care
put it over there.

> *Hey,*
> *that rhymes.*

Wait,
> *what did I say?*

I didn't
    hear
        my
            self.

Kitchen conversations after twenty years of marriage. (Resultant poem sounds forlorn, but we were actually laughing a lot.)

My Place

It fills me with great pleasure
to know my place,
where stories slip
from behind gray clouds
on shafts of sunlight
and vultures rise on silent wings
from misty valleys.
Where root and stone
and stone and root
entwine,
so it is no longer possible
to tell who
supports
who.
Where hawks drop
from blue skies
to settle on oaken boughs
before my eyes
and snakes slide
between dry leaves.
Where I know how maple leaves
catch the sunshine
and hickory leaves
hold raindrops
and the frosted red canes

of wild raspberry curve
and arc across morning,
small buds
nestling with summer promise
against unfurled leaves.
Where trees yield ground
to mushrooms and moss
and crows trace familiar paths
along the skyline.
Where I may sit in a green cocoon
in the palm of the
forest
watching
so still and silent
that when I finally swallow
the sound startles me.
There is so much rapture
to be found in
knowing my place that
for a moment,
I've forgotten
all
my
edges.

For Tom Johnson.

An Ocean of Wholeness

The morning mist curls
from the valley
into shafts of sunlight
and thin single strands
of spider's web
stretch from tree to tree
like fairy clotheslines.
The rain drenched moss
sighs over stones,
riotous anticipation
fills the blackberry blooms,
and oak branches dip beneath
the small weights of
squirrels and mockingbirds.
I lay on my back
on cold stone
watching wispy white clouds
drift across the sky
and
remembering
there is an ocean
of wholeness
all around.

Reminder

*You are not
one relentless
self-improvement
project.*

*You are a marvel
of art and fire
and the world
is in your eyes.*

Earth Crone

She has gathered
seeds and stories
and woven them
into her cloak of power.
She weaves the wind
and watches the watchers.
She listens to storms
and sighs,
crowcall
and leafshadow.
She knows
this earth
through belly
bones
and blood.

Unseen

This morning
sun spangled
silver teardrops
of rain
laced through
the cedars.
The horizon line
has faded out of sight
under a canopy of green
and I have become too
small to see out
of this burgeoning,
song-laden
cocoon of life
even when I stand
on a big rock.
There are times for
being far-seeing
and times for being
unseen so
I nestle
into the palm of the forest
watching squirrels
and listening to turkeys

until it is time
to duck beneath wet
hickory branches
and follow the mossy path
back home.

Keep Singing

You do not have to give
everything away
or share every scrap
of insight
in order to be real.
You can nestle some
stories
and some silence
right under your breast.
Shh, shh, it's okay,
drink deeply of life
and what you have made from it.
This is your weaving.
This is your blood.
This is your pain.
This is your truth.
This is your song.
Remember to keep singing.

Your Story

You have a story
worth telling.
To decide you are
interesting enough
to write about,
learn from,
study,
and explore
is
a
radical
act.

Building

I want to build my life
from canes
of wildberry and wonder,
planes of stone,
and layers of meaning,
angles of sunlight,
and shafts of shadow,
spangles of raindrop
on spider's web
and cedar.
I want to build my life
from river,
vine,
root,
and stone
until each breath
is a prayer
and every step
is a miracle.
I will live my poems,
sweat my prayers,
and let devotion
sweep me away
to a place where tears,

love,
and longing
entwine
into one
whole
life.

Attachment

If this is attachment,
I welcome it,
as the roots
welcome the rain.

If this is hope,
I'll feel it,
because the last thing
the world needs
is more people who
have given up on hope.

If this is magic,
I'll know it,
because I can feel
my heartbeat
in my wrist.

If this is wonder,
I'll share it,
because it is wondering
that we wander into ourselves.

If this is mystery,

I'll hold it,
because deep inside,
the mystery waving back
tells me it is what weaves
this world together.

If this is delight,
I'll savor it,
because in clinging to
abstractions
about meaning and matter
I'll miss it.

If this is longing,
I'll let it,
because it is in
moving with the river of desire
that we grow new wings
and set our souls aflame.

If this is fear,
I'll claim it,
because it is talking to the shadows
that we make friends with life.

If this is patience,
I'll practice it,
because it is in witnessing,
that we find out what
we've been asking all along.

If this is devotion,
I'll name it,
because it is in persistent noticing
that enchantment seeps into our souls and
skin.

If this is joy,
I'll dance with it,
for we need never decline
an invitation
to feel alive.

If this is wisdom,
I'll whisper it,
for the world
is full of voices,
waiting to be heard.

The Cliffs of Questioning

What if there is more
than enough time
for your unbound dreams?
What if there is also time
to build a tabernacle
for tears
and to weave strands
of the ordinary
into your own holy text?
What if there is way
to dance prayers into being,
limits into loving,
hope into forever?
What if there is a path
to be carved through
an endless landscape
of mystery
in the mystical terrain
right behind your eyes?
What if you scrape your joy
back out of the canyon
of longing
and watch it soar
outside your edges?

What if you scale cliffs
of the imaginary
and discover your power
is perched within your reach
and it has been smiling at you
all along?
What if you are more than you know,
less lost than you fear,
and whole
in your center?

For Agnes Vojta.

Gooseberry Morning

I set aside my roaming
through arid and infertile
mental terrain
and step barefoot from
stone to stone
until I feel deconstriction
in my mind.
Then I put on my shoes
and follow gooseberries
into the woods,
a humid
green cathedral
of quiet
where I crouch and peer
under leaves
patiently
awaiting round berries
to become visible
as my eyes adjust their focus
to that which is needed to
see the patterns made
by green against green.
It is both a softening
and a sharpening
that is needed

before green globes
swim into view.
Where before
there was "nothing,"
there is something
now
for patient eyes to discover.
Gooseberries are shy berries,
tucked beneath their green
umbrellas,
unlike the showy invitation
of raspberries
leaning rapturously into the sun.
Wild raspberries ask for fortitude of skin
and courage of reach,
but gooseberries require coaxing,
stillness,
and surrender
before seeing.
Life too,
requires a combination
of all these things,
wildberry lessons
for living.

Hope

Do not despair
or lose hope
for there is a place
where hawks swoop low
over waving oaks,
three crows trace a path
across a white moon,
grasses nod their heads
in the sunlight,
and roses bloom
all by themselves.

In the Temple of the Ordinary

In the temple
of the ordinary
on the altar
of the every day,
Life laid before me
a worn cup of turtle shell
upon a mossy stump,
a shiny black crow's feather
across brown gravel,
and two red-shouldered hawks
twirling together across
white clouds.
In the temple
of the ordinary
on the altar
of the everyday,
Life laid before me
my own living wholeness
and luckily
I was listening.

Re-Collection

I set out to re-collect myself
to rebuild my spirit
and to reweave my dreams.
I moved through an underworld
of my own making
and a canyon
of my own confusion
up a ladder of self-doubt
and despair.
One foot in front of the other
I continued
until upon a slab
of lichen covered stone
I took a deep breath
and discovered
the breath
the heart
the stone
were all made of wonder.
Mystery and magic
piled together
with a scoop of tears,
a pang of boredom,
a tendril of regret,

a wave of feeling
all in a cauldron of being.
We do not become whole
by thinking ourselves
through to an answer
or in finally figuring it all out
and never questioning again.
We find our wholeness by
watching the world move
with our arms wide open
and realizing that we are each,
in every moment,
already whole,
already redeemed.

It is into that stillpoint
of being present
that we must continue to
trust, see, and know
as we whisper
one more promise
to the wind.

Song: Elemental

I am a wonder
of mud and magic
heartbeat walking
through waking worlds

I am a breath
of ancient knowing
ancestors calling
across the seas

I am a marvel
of art and fire
and my wings
are wide and wise

I am a weaving
of words and water
moonstained mysteries
and sunsoaked dreams.

I am a mystery
of blood and power
windspun spells
and unbound prayers.

I am a song
of earth and wonder
sunrise passion
and cauldron's fire.

Surprise

I am marveling at the
endless mysteries
possible on a
single patch of ground
watching four vultures glide
across the valley
and feeling the sprinkle
of leftover rain across my shoulders
when I hear a noise
and turn to see
a mother raccoon
and three roly-poly babies
standing on the rock behind me
only about twelve inches away.
Our eyes meet and I know
the surprise in her eyes
because I feel the same
expression in my own.
You are not a rock,
her eyes say.
You are not a cat,
mine reply.

Meaning

The world is alive with meaning.
I can hear it in a thousand heartbeats.
I can see it on a thousand wings.
I can touch it in a thousand flowers.
I can taste it in a single, wild mulberry
hanging red-black
in the sun-striped green shadows.
It is sweet.

Message from Morning

It is okay to pause,
breathe,
and be
while the world keeps
turning
beneath your feet.

Balm

The balm I need from my depths
is a sweet expanse
of uncommitted time,
a deep breath down to my toes,
a sweep of my arms to the sky
a slice of silent witnessing
of just
what
is.
To know surprise
and delight is as close
as the front door
and to step open-handed
into the sun.
The balm I need from my depths is
permission to pause,
watch,
notice,
and not know.
May I lie on my back in the clover
watch a crow soar over head
and know myself as worthy
of time.

Building Materials

When I determined
it was time
to rebuild my soul,
I set out to do it
using the materials
available to me
in my own back yard:
trees,
stones,
birds,
sunlight,
moss,
and morning.

News

Often the news is full
of sorrow,
but I am here to tell you
that wild foxglove
blankets an abandoned meadow
with beauty.

Roaming

*I want to roam
the woodlands
for timeless hours
until I shelve
all my questions
and know only
the beat
of my own heart
as holy and true.*

Wild Night

Mist blankets the hills
and valley,
a lone deer
watches from a green field,
and two doves rise up
across the trees.
Without warning,
in the gloaming,
a wild chorus of coyotes
begins to howl.
The sounds of
three different packs
in three directions
encircles us in an eerie cone
of song
under a slender sickle
of moon in a sun-striped sky.
Part of me feels like howling too
a guest on the grounds
of a wild night.

Wild Eyes

On a green morning
in the palm of the forest
in a cocoon made of
countless leaves
I watched three baby raccoons
attempt to scale an oak tree
while their mother gazed
from a nearby limb.
She kept watchful eyes
upon me
with a crooning growl of caution
as the babies tumbled through
the leaves
gathering in one fluffy bunch
upon the branch beside her.
I returned to my stone
peering quietly through the underbrush
into black-masked eyes
when I heard a noise behind me
and turned to see a lone coyote
loping through the woods
only ten feet away.
I continued to sit
in silent surprise

at these close encounters
of the exact right time,
sharing one terrain
of landscape and being.
A hawk began to call,
I could still taste wild raspberry
on my tongue,
and pollen drifting by
illuminated into dancing sparkles
by a shaft of sunlight
reminded me
that we are all made
of a thousand
invisible
things.

Hobbled

Who are you without your symbols
and your striving
when you are ragged in your skin?
Who are you when you are stripped bare,
laid raw,
unknowing and alone?
How do you know how to rise
when you have fallen,
fly when you are hobbled,
and soar when you ache?
Where might you soak
in a deep pool of truth
until your bones knit back together
and you rise shivering into
a moonlit night
full of fire?
Can you scoop hope back into your arms
re-collect yourself from where you've fallen
gather your tattered edges
and lay down new seams
with bright threads of possibility?
Can you shed your skin,
cast off your longing,
spread your wings,

and steep your meaning
into a strong,
sweet
concoction
of renewed truth,
purpose,
and vision?
Can you lay it all down
and then pick up what you still want
and re-weave your heart,
truth,
spirit
with lumps, bumps, passion, and power
all entwined?

Loosen My Limits

On a gentle morning,
without expectations
without force,
the wind sweeps by
and a patter of stored raindrops
cascades to the forest floor
from the canopy of green leaves.
A cloud of mist rises
into the shafts of sunlight
filtering through the trees,
forming a shimmering wisp
hanging tenuously in the air,
a mystic portal,
an otherworldly gateway
in the trees.
I watch until it drifts away,
enchanted by this tiny moment
of morning.
I wonder,
as I have before,
what would happen
if I kept sitting
and followed beyond,
into an entire day.

If I can spot so much magic
in slender slices of morning,
what might I see in the rest of the day?
I don't know if I could even hold it.
To think that more is possible,
makes me feel both small and powerful.
To dig deeper,
stay longer,
see more,
might explode me,
deconstruct my edges,
loosen my limits,
transform certainty into ecstasy,
melt me into stone,
spiders dripping
from my lichen covered shoulders
and coming to rest
on the raindrops
in my center.

Living Truth

I want to saturate myself
in wild streams
of living truth.
I want to dance my spirit
into the whirling heart
of desire.
I want to soak my soul
in a river
of unbound dreams.
I want to lace ribbons
of wonder
and tendrils of hope
through my blood.
I want to twine layers
of loving through
my fingertips
and around my center.
I want to shape my life
through wings and walks.
I want to carve my path
through canyons of curiosity
and caverns of peace.
I want to weave my destiny
from the fibers

of poems and passions.
I want to collect strands
and stories
of soul-waking
and coil them into
nourishing soil
where they can grow into
unquenchable amazement.
I want to sear infinite
tracings of beauty
across my heart
and pierce my palms
with the endless miracle
of being alive.

Summer

Remember:
You, too,
need sun
and rain
to bloom.

Summer Muse

*I listen to the
summer's song,
the sweet blessing
of water's flow,
the sweep of wind
through branches
reaching for the sun,
the exuberant spread
of blossoms
across sweet meadows
and rocky slopes,
the dance of sunlight
and shadow
with white clouds
and radiant growth.
Across fields delighting
with daisies
and into valleys
swaying with wildberries
and indigo longing,
my heart beats
with the tempo
of the everyday magic
of this world.*

*In the temple of
the ordinary
the extraordinary
tapestry of being
is woven.*

Rose Lessons

There are blooms and brambles
in every day,
in every life.
You will need both softening
and striving,
patience and pushing,
delight and determination,
to move through your living
under sunshine and thunder.
May both tenderness
and fierceness
be your guides.

The Wild Heart Wonders

Shh...
Place your hand on your wild heart
What does she have to say?
Listen.

Does she whisper of longings
for sacred spaces,
meadows of dreams,
acres of promise,
mountains of meaning?
Does she sing of cool pools,
wandering trails,
tall peaks,
and firelit meeting places?
Does she howl for love
and a deep craving
to finally be heard?
Does she know exactly what you need?
Can you allow her time to speak?

Wild Heart Responds

My wild heart whispers
of clovered meadows,
silent stones,
and outstretched wings
across the skies.
She tells of time.
Time for sunlight
across closed eyelids
and sweet swaths
of supine pleasure.
She feels at home
in fallen leaves
and mossy expanses,
trickling streams
and windswept shores.
She dreams of just
sitting still
with nothing else
to
do.

Miracles

What if you
live a miracle
every
single
day
and you don't even
have to
earn it?

On the Brink

One day you will find yourself
teetering on the brink
forked tongue tasting the air
and eyes full of fire.
It is good to be alive and breathing
on the precipice of change.

World Ceremonies

Sometimes the world weaves
ceremonies for us
without us needing
to design them,
or plan them.
Rather we need only show up
with awareness
and witness the ritual
as it unfolds.

For Barbara Johnson.

Inspiration Wanders

When inspiration wanders away
I am left with what is now,
breathing into cramped space,
a slice of morning,
filled with voices,
while the hawk's call rises to a wild,
feverish pitch
across white clouds in a blue sky.

Offering: Cauldron Keeper

Listen.
I am
the cauldron-keeper.
I breathe fire
into the night,
coax coals
into souls,
and tend the flame
of eternal mystery.
I hear.
I hold.
I am.

Offering: Moonwatcher

Listen.
I am
the moonwatcher
I have breathed
the breath of stars
and watched
new
worlds whirl
into being.
I hear.
I hold.
I am.

Rebuilding the Web

I knelt by creamy
white pokeberry flowers
each forming a small cup
that will tenderly cradle
a poisonous blue-black berry
by August.
I am charmed to see
a delicate web woven there,
a tiny, nearly transparent spider
in the center
in a poignant representation
of interconnection.
Suddenly, the figurine I set
by the blooms tips and falls,
caught only by a single poke leaf
and teetering suspended
over thorny ground.
The movement of the leaf
tears the web
and I feel a pang of shock
to see this easy destruction
of harmony.
But, as I watch,
in the space

of one shaking breath,
the tiny spider,
translucent and alone,
gathers one shining thread
and slowly,
gracefully,
without hesitation
begins
rebuilding
what is damaged.

Blue Heron

I love living on land
where the great blue herons
glide on strong, steady wings
across cotton candy clouds
trailing through the sky
at sunset's end
while fireflies wink
through wildberry leaves
on a deepening summer night.

Trust

Maybe it is possible to
just trust yourself;
the rhythm of your days,
the ebb and flow of inspiration,
the continued unfolding of your life
as it occurs,
step by step,
day by day,
breath by breath.

Wild Blueberries

On a humid morning,
feeling stale and crumbled
I crept through spiderwebs
and under green branches
onto flat stones,
where a tall poke plant
greeted me
red-purple and majestic
in the sun-dappled shadows.
From a lowbush blueberry
I picked five blue-black berries
and ate a single one slowly
as a red-shouldered hawk
raised its cry from the depths.
I felt a rush of wild joy,
a sense of exhilaration,
and delight
with this,
the first time in forty years
that I've found a wild blueberry
in the woods and eaten it.
I stood barefoot in the leaves
sweat on my brow,
and the taste of wild blueberry

on my tongue
and fell in love, again,
with this world,
with my life,
with these woods.
How miraculous
that so much can change
in the space of
five
small
blueberries.

For John Stuckey.

In Summary

Keep getting up
in the morning.
Keep loving the way
the sun shines.
Keep being surprised
and delighted
by the landscape of colors
as the wheel turns.
Keep looking for birds,
for they carry magic
across the sky right to your eyes.
Listen for moonlight.
Turn your head when
you hear a branch crack.
Talk to crows.
Spend time with hawks.
Converse with wild berries of all kinds
for they hold whole
fields of possibility
beneath their skins.
If rain falls, let it soak.
Laugh with the thunder.
Whisper prayers
and promises to the wind.

Cry under rainbows.
Sing to clouds.
And let the wildflowers
of the roadsides
teach you what it means to live.

There is Nothing Tidy Here

There is nothing tidy here
life is too broad and billowing
to be contained,
restrained,
confined,
constrained
by lists and wishes
and well-laid plans,
or even by thin and bloodless prayers.
There is nothing tidy here,
expect wild winds and sharp teeth
amid the violets and sunrises.
There is nothing tidy here,
the world a great jumble
of twining grapevines,
sprawling brambles,
winding roots,
and beating hearts.
There is nothing to do
with such an untidy world,
but whirl with the wonder of it all,
keeping your hand outstretched
to touch everything,
even if your feet bleed
and your skin is streaked
with sorrow and joy.

At the Gates

I dreamed I practiced yoga
at the Gates of Mordor
rolling my purple mat
out carefully on parched
and barren ground.
Balancing on one leg
I extended my hand across
a fiery and forbidden horizon,
leg arching backward
into dancer's pose,
the quintessential
pose of destination yogis.
Finding my center
even while
facing
Mount Doom.

Behind the Curtain

I have a temple
in the secret spaces
of my heart.
Within it, I worship
the white-green waxy canes
of first-year raspberries
arching high to kiss
the weathered boards of the deck.
I relish the sharp cries of the hawks
rising over the creaking groan
of the cicadas.
I cherish the way the lightning bugs
nestle asleep
beneath curled mulberry leaves
waiting for twilight.
Here in the secret temple
of my heart,
behind the curtain
in the holy of the holies
I discover my own shining face
looking out into the day
with love in my eyes.
I hear the quick, watery call
of a red cardinal in green cedar,

an indigo bunting
glowing rich and blue
as it sways lightly
on a stalk of wild lettuce.
Feeling the soft breeze
that strokes my shoulders
without needing anything from me,
the bones of my own truth
right below the clouds.
The soft thrum of blood
through my being
twines prayers
beneath my tendons
and I savor
the taut skin
of a wild blueberry,
the purple puff
of a ironweed bloom.

Inspired by a writing prompt in the Oasis
from Jennifer Louden.

Ranging

Do not store anger
in your tender breast,
the soft territory of your humanity
requires room to roam.
Let yourself range through
landscapes of pain and joy
until you weave together
a cloak of power.
Let buried grief rise up
and spill over onto
sunstreaked ground
until it soaks away.
Breathe in and know
you are whole.
Breathe out and know
you are here.
Sit with everything
until you know
what you need to do.
The answers are there,
waiting beneath
your thin and magic
skin.

Courage

We cannot be seduced
into despair by fear.
We must live out loud,
with our arms open
to the moon,
the sun,
the rain,
and the whirling wonder of it all.

Untidy Magic

There is magic to be found
in an untidy life,
in an untidy world
where nothing stays the same
and growth
is always possible.

Preparing to Exhale

The year is beginning to exhale.
The peaking growth of summer
beginning to breathe out,
to slow,
to ripen,
to dry,
to fold inward,
to go to seed,
preparing for a season of rest.

Message from Midsummer

You can have...
Space to breathe.
Room to think.
Freedom of choice.
Time for joy.

Inhale.
Exhale.

From the Spaces

I am from the spaces between
time
in which diamond raindrops speak,
and from the holes
in the fabric of reality
that stretch to hold everything
and yield when necessary to the confines
of blood and breath,
remaining always available
in seams of dreams
and shreds of devotion.
I am from acres of mud,
stone, and thorns,
berries full of space
and magic
ripe
for the plucking.
I am here for knowing
though I come from
nothing
into
now.

Witnessing without Fixing

You don't need to fix anything,
it is okay to let your feelings feel,
to let your swoops swoop,
to let your not-knowing not-know,
to let your hope soar
and then plummet,
to let your joy be joyful,
to let your tears be hot.

Witnessing,
without fixing.

Message from Midday

If you are always waiting
for time
to just be,
perhaps that means
it is time to
just
be.

AND

If you are always waiting
for time
to finally rest,
perhaps that means
it is time to
finally
rest.

Morning Glory Magic

I knelt in a surprise
of morning glories
wild, white, and wonderful,
springing up between
gray stones
on a gravel road,
the concerns of the hour
drifting away on curls
of wind and crowcall.
Descending into the present,
my world becomes as small
and as large as a delicate cup of petals
blushed with pink.
A black feather rests on the stones
and a hawk cries
over the western valley.
When I finally blink and rise
back into the day
my legs cramped
from my roadside devotional
I feel I have been transported
to another plane
through the simply radical
act
of noticing.

Liminal Moment

In a pause between
morning and magic
wait at the threshold,
held between
crow and rabbit,
feeling yourself in liminal space
between earth and sky,
between movement and breath,
expectant,
alert,
poised in times
between time,
and then,
take another step
into the weeds and wonder
of your own why.

Bloodland

Some may say my world
is too small,
the size of a square deck,
a field of waving grasses and wildflowers,
a strip of brown and gray gravel road,
a tiny temple shrouded in oak leaves,
roses,
and incense.
How can you learn everything
you need to know from
a grove of trees,
a bowl of blue sky,
a patch of earth woven
of roots and stones.
This is my bloodland
and to me
it shines
with an infinite universe
of small stories.

For Barbara and Tom Johnson.

This Much is Up to You

You may choose
whether or not
to dance
with your life,
sunstreaked, awestriped,
ragged, and strong
on the changing edges
of a mysterious world.
This much is up to you.

Combleaf

They may call you false foxglove,
but I call you beautiful.
Forget about defining yourself
by what you're not,
and keep reaching
open-hearted
toward the sun.

Elemental Gifts

I followed three crows of morning
into an otherworld of Now,
branches arching over
gravel road into a tunnel
of discovery.
On my sojourn
I encountered three gifts:
from Air, a vulture feather
ragged and silent
though I can feel the flight
left in it.
From Earth, a sickle of rusted metal,
perhaps a worn horseshoe,
perhaps a relic of 125 horsepower.
From Fire, six morning glory
blossoms curled into tight flames of pink
that only open to the right amount of light.
I tried to find a snail shell, from Water,
to complete my perfect quartet,
but the more I looked,
the less I found.
If there is anything I've learned
it is that magic unfolds on its own,
no forcing needed.

To Be a Hag

I will be a hag and love it
reclaiming that sharp and spiny title
from the thorns and stones and flames
of history
and reweaving herstory
in a hag's cabin in the forest,
walls twined with vines and stories,
healing and power bubbling
together in a vat above the fire.
My eyes will grow bright with age,
hair twirled like snakes
and spiders dripping
from my shoulders,
a tea cup in my hand
steeping forbidden wisdom
for breakfast.
I will roll soft leaves
of mullein into tapers
drench them in beeswax
and light them, grinning,
under a full golden moon.
I will be the bright-moon walker,
the hill strider,
the hedge and edge rider,

the starshower,
the web-knower.
Beneath hackberry,
blackberry,
mulberry and stone,
I will coax deep strands
of witnessing
from silence,
shells and bone.

Message from Wild Skullcap

*Be both tender
and tenacious.
Rise strong from
where you have drifted.
Heal where you can.*

Faith

I have faith in myself
to spot morning glories
twining tender and tenacious
across stony ground
and to crawl on my knees
if it is needed
to access beauty.
I have faith in myself
to breathe in the rain
and sleep in the night,
to find two varieties
of evening primrose
along a single mile
of roadway
and to love each one
like it is a treasure.
I have faith in myself
to hear whispers from the forest
and songs carried by wings
on the wind.
I have faith in myself
to stop and stare
into the unbridled enchantment
of this everyday world.

I have faith in myself
to alight on my true desires
with as much skill, care, and grace
as a blue swallowtail butterfly
waves on a purple thistle
under a morning sky.

Trust

Because I trust myself,
this week
I will follow crows,
study butterflies,
learn from wild yellow foxglove
and slender bush clover.
I will make eye contact with a deer,
veins tracing rivers along
the narrow triangle of her face,
and with the turtle crossing the road
face speckled with orange, white, and black.
I will take long, grateful strides across stony
ground
and watch for copperhead snakes
on brown stones.
I will breathe humid air,
complain about bug bites
as blood streaks my shins
and delight again and again
in living on a land
that brings me face to face
with awe
every day.

Last Night

I watched nine crows
glide over the lake
nasal conversations echoing
across the water
as tendrils of mist rose
into the trees.
Glowing white moons
of bindweed flowers
twined like holiday lights
through the ivy
and a snapping turtle
rose up prehistoric
from the algae
to look for snacks.
A quick flash of movement
alerted me to a red-brown snake
swimming whip-like along
the shallow shoreline.
And, as the sky faded to night,
the shadowy black and white form
of a skunk
trundled fluffy and noiseless
across our path.
I have no flash of insight or revelation,

no streak of inspiration
or pithy life lesson to share,
but I will tell you
that delicate fingers of mist
continue to drift upward
joining tree to cloud.

Message from Mushroom

You will know
when the time is right to emerge.
Draw nourishment
from shadowed and secret places.
There is much more than you know
below the surface.
Seize opportunities for flourishing
when they come.
Remember there is a whole world
of unseen magic
right beneath your feet.

(Optional: keep people guessing about
whether or not you're poisonous!)

For Mike and Cara Snyder (who are not
poisonous!)

Message from Chicory

Bloom while you can.
Trust your roots.
Turn your face to the sun.
Do not settle for being a substitute,
honor the full flavor of who you are.

Questions

Questions for a night
in which the earth
is pregnant with dreams:
What are you seeking?
How are you listening?
What is your living truth?

Thin Magic

I chose not to follow crows today,
but turned away
to follow the mist instead,
descending down a rocky hill
and into an underworld of my own making,
in which I laid aside
the pressures of pleasantness
and considered how it would feel
to lay my drive down too
across the stones
and walk away,
leaving it gasping in surrender
between a flattened cracker of frog
and finality.
I knelt beside blue chicory
with a cloak of white fog across my shoulders
feeling weary of smiling,
thin of patience,
and with only a thread of faded magic
beating feebly beneath my skin.
I pondered messages from purple asters,
gravel beneath my knees,
and resisted reaching for rosehips
through an ebbing bower of poison ivy.

An unripe persimmon, gleaming purple-red
below the bright white sky,
rolled into my path
and as I made my way back up the hill
two vultures rose silent and hulking from the
trees,
so close I heard their feathers whispering
together.
I felt an ember quicken quietly
beneath my breast
and on the gliding motion of broad wings,
I was reminded that we
can always
choose which way to go,
and that even thin
and tattered magic
is worth
savoring.

September Staleness

This is the staleness
of September,
dust rising up
from tired ground.
Worn brown stars
are still beautiful though,
crisped and complete,
hearts open in surrender
as their work ends.

Soaring

I dreamed of newborn twin fawns
in a shady forest
wobbly legs carrying them
through the trees.
In reality, this morning
twin fawns,
no longer newborn,
but still spotted,
crop grass with their mother
in the field across the road.
I approach with quiet care
head lowered so as not to threaten,
but as I draw parallel
they catch my eyes with theirs
and flee
white flags waving
as they snort and blow away
into the shelter of the trees.
As I descend the hill,
five vultures
soar above me,
wingtips seeming to
skim the treetops
as I shelter in a green colonnade,

head tilted,
body still.
They look like speed skaters
as they swoop and glide
with practiced ease across the clouds.
Something in my heart loosens
as I watch them fly,
a piece of it yearning,
or already knowing,
what it feels like to soar.
The wind carries a distinctive
bleachy tang
to my weak human nose
and it occurs to me
that I actually like
being the kind of person
who recognizes
the smell of vultures
on the wing.

Autumn

*Between the shadow
and the shine,
there is a place
that needs your time.*

Autumn Muse

Listen.
I am autumn's song,
the glow of the setting sun,
the abundance of the harvest,
the rich savoring of wonder,
and the wisdom of
letting things go.
I tell of falling leaves
and riversong,
sparks rising into twilight,
and the taste of honey
and cinnamon upon the tongue.
In the whispers of branches,
the bend of grains
beneath the sun,
the ember glow
of restoration,
satisfaction,
and satiation,
I find the secrets
of my self
and soul.

A Fierce Reminder

I am propelled by a fierce passion.
I am fueled by a fierce magic.
I am inspired by a fierce purpose.
I am carried by a fierce love.
I am awakening to a fierce trust
in my own fire.

Wild Grass

I am in love
with the wild grasses
of morning
and the way sunlight
rests on seed and stem.

Fall Balance

We are balanced
at the centerpoint
of change,
the stillpoint
between breaths,
the crossroads
of being,
watching as Persephone
draws away,
trailing golden light
across the hills
and the earth exhales
before the deepening
begins.

Scaling Nets in Roller Skates

I dreamed I was traversing
an obstacle course
wearing roller skates
while scaling a net
strung over a warehouse floor.
I reached the top and looked down
to see Mark below me.
He lifted the net and simply
rolled under it
saying: "I don't do things
that are difficult,
only to be difficult."
There is a metaphor
for life here,
a depiction of a marriage,
and a Zen lesson for living,
all bound together in one dream.
But, I also take a moment
to celebrate being the woman
willing to scale a net in roller skates
if she thinks that is what is needed.
In life, there are nets that must be climbed,
our wheels spinning
across the air,

and there are nets that can be lifted
as we roll away on solid ground.
May we remember to practice exquisite
discernment and
may we know that
multiple ways of moving
through the world are
always possible.

Space

May you make a space for wondering,
carving it out of hollows
between root and stone.
May you make a space for wandering,
ranging over lands
striped with sunlight and shadow.
May you make a space for witnessing,
learning from wild grasses
and silent wings.
May you make a space for magic,
as she threads enchantment
through your bones and veins.
And, may you come to trust forever
the whispered spells
that weave and waver
right beneath
the tender knowing in your skin.

Crossroads in Autumn

At the crossroads,
wild white asters
have filled the center,
and alluring grasses
are incandescent with sunlight.
Sometimes we don't
have to choose which way to go,
but can wait
at the center point of change
listening to the wind.

Don't Ignore the Light

Don't pass by
the slender shafts
of sunlight
that catch your eye,
stop in the temple
of the ordinary
and pray
holding sunshine
and shadows
in your open hands.

A Bloom

Wild purple asters
have sprouted up
in abundance
by the temple
and a single red rose
is beside them,
heavy, open, glowing
as rain spatters
through the trees
onto grateful stems.
My thoughts feel
parched and weary,
brittle and splintered
and yet
somewhere inside
I can
sense
a bloom.

Scraps of Succor for the Soul from the Shores of Despair

When the weariness finds you,
when you wonder whether you've
got anything left to give,
when you are heartsick, heartsore,
and worn in your bones...

Gather the shreds of your soul
and knit them back together
with the needles of longing.
Collect the shards of your spirit,
and mosaic together a living truth
that shines through every crack.
Crawl through the stones and stems
until you find the shades of joy
that you thought you'd lost,
and hold them up to the sun.
Patiently unpick the snarls of your striving
and run your hands over
the fibers of your being
until you can feel
the knots loosen
and the heart beneath them

shift and soar.
Gather the grit and gravel of living
and sift it until it sparkles
with the sweetness of
renewed wonder.
Slide your hands through slivers
of meaning until you find
the scraps that hold
your secrets
even if they slice a bit
and are sharp to taste.
Watch your shadows sneak past you
while you snack on strips of sorrow
and sip spicy
draughts of delight.
Sink into surprise,
letting the wind curl
around your shoulders
to stroke your spine.
Soften into wildness
as life strips you back into splinters
and slows your steps.
Slip into the stream of living,
scooping up the knowing

that refuses to be silenced
and bow before
the swell of understanding
that promises to keep you afloat
and swimming
on the spirals and swirls of this,
life's sacred song.

Slow Magic

I watched a herd of teenage boys
during track practice at the park,
thin and straining,
they ran with a loud-voiced coach
shouting at them, exhorting them
to go faster, to be better.
You are not fast enough, he screamed,
you have wasted this whole day.
I skirted around them
and rolled across acorns to the lake
where I sat on a bench
with a duck on my left
and a chipmunk on my right.
The half moon hung low and heavy,
pale silver in a denim sky
and across the lake
between the trees,
I saw a cemetery full of people who
may have been too fast or too slow,
we'll never know.
The duck's green head is shiny in the sun
and as I watch, its eyes slowly close
and it naps while the chipmunk
eyes me steadily, silent and still as a stone.

Behind me I can hear harsh
men's voices,
the boys' feet on gravel.
There is nothing wrong with pushing yourself,
with not giving up,
but I think too of the women
at Red Tent and their
sometimes weary faces,
no longer remembering how to rest,
starving for time and self,
and reclaiming their right to say
enough,
no more.
It is okay to stop,
to slow down,
really.
I remember the men on the army base
on which I used to teach,
who asked me to help them
learn how to feel again,
and I remember how radical,
how revolutionary,
how impossibly simple it is,
to go slowly,

to take a break,
to listen your body,
to rest when you need to,
to trust your heart,
and even,
to give up if you want to,
letting your head dip in the sun,
as shadows play across the water
and the wind blows
through white headstones.
There is much in the world that screams
at us for speed
and few things that will ever
ask us to be slower.
I look over at the chipmunk,
but it has slipped away.
In its place a giant snail shell
lies quietly across the stones.
May we pay attention to the
slow magic
at our shores.

For my children.

Possibility

If you feel you've lost your way,
listen,
and let yourself remember.
Watch,
and let yourself know.
Explore,
and let yourself trust.
Each day holds the possibility
to weave conscious experience anew.

No Forced Magic

No forced magic,
no forced smiles,
just sunlight across
green-brown water
and wind rippling
through cypress branches.
A smell like bad breath
lifts off the ripples,
but if you sit upwind,
with your back against a tree,
you can pretend everything
is healthy.
Two curious turtles
poke their blade-like heads
above the surface,
a dragonfly skims by,
and a bright orange
monarch butterfly
coasts delicately across the clouds.
A groundhog waddles on the bank,
a duck passes by,
and the wind catches the cattails
while roaring motors
echo from the roadway.

This bubble of living
containing both
stink and shore
cattail and roar.

Behind the Sunrise

The day rippled with scarlet fire
below gray layers of warning
and three osprey glided
over the waves,
white bellies lit pink
with a blush of light,
wings black blades against
a thunderous morning.
We watched a woman wade
into the water,
full-figured and resplendent
in a bright flower-strewn bikini.
As she gazed at the horizon,
six dolphins circled in front of her,
a modern Venus rising
from the shells and surf,
wind in her hair,
as their silver tails slapped the water.
Across the sand,
shining black crows whirled around
a tall pink clock tower,
cawing into the dawn.
There is a simple magic,
in secret strips of time
behind the sunrise.

Sometimes

Sometimes you find a song
laid out across the stones.
Sometimes you learn a story
as it echoes through your bones.
Sometimes you pluck a prayer
from strands of open air.
Sometimes with blood and thread
you weave something new to share.
Sometimes you carry poems
across shells onto the shore.
Sometimes you ache for beauty
and cry out for something more.
Sometimes you walk with wonder,
mixing magic with your tears.
Sometimes you run from thunder
and shelter in your fears.
Always you have your breath,
your heart,
and open hands.
May you live in hope and wholeness
and make friends
with wind and sand.

Message: Sing Your Song

Don't forget to sing
your own songs.
Don't let them fade
from your soul and skin.
Let them deepen and ripen
and bite sharply,
straight into the center of life,
startling you back to reality
in this world that you love,
on this land that you need,
in this life that you crave,
in this heart that you know.

Where Joy Lives

There is a place
where joy lives.
Find it.

There is a place
where hope dwells.
Seek it.

There is a place
where love shelters.
Share it.

There is a place
where you will be
cracked open
wholly whole and holy.
Trust it.

Moonrise Over the Atlantic

In the hour in which
day and night meet
and meld
the pumpkin moon
laid down a path
of golden light
across the water,
as it slipped above the horizon,
full,
orange,
glowing
like a surprising sunrise
at night.
It lifted silently into
a nest of clouds
and sheltered there
in a rosy cup
of twilight,
round,
luminous,
and certain of its own talent
for making waves.

Time Unspooled

There is so much to remember,
to write down,
to fix in the mind,
and yet time continues to spin
and in the ebb and flow of experiencing
even trying to fix it down,
to hold onto it,
means you're missing
something else,
something new.
The swoop of fish crows against
the water
wings black silk in the sun,
the surprising orange bloom of a monarch
butterfly
swaying in the wind over
the waves of the Atlantic,
the swift sweep of an osprey
spreading wide wings in a flock of brown
pelicans,
white under-feathers flashing,
the joy I feel as I watch my sons in the surf
poignantly aware that this is
the only day in my life

in which I will watch these tall teenage boys
playing in the waves in just this way.
Only this,
only now,
the sharp thin shoulders of a
five year old boy
striding ahead of me over a curved wooden
bridge,
the soft sand beneath my palms
as I close my hands and feel
each grain
gently swirl away
from my grip.
The water rolls,
my heart beats,
and it all passes by.
Time unspooled
for a flash of now
in salt and sun.

Living Your Poems

Sometimes poems wait
just beyond your reach
below the surface of your skin,
beyond the shore,
on a distant horizon,
behind the trees or clouds.

Sometimes they wait
to be picked up,
plucked from between
roots and stones,
carved out of memory
and the spaces between thoughts.

Sometimes they coast by
on outstretched wings
waiting for your lifted hands
to catch a feather
or a shadow.

Sometimes they whisper
on the wind
echoing through
mulberry leaves

and slipping off rose petals
and onto raindrops.

Sometimes they weave by
with silver threads of moonlight
and spiderwebs
or with golden filaments spinning
between seed and scale.

Sometimes they flutter,
sometimes they soar,
sometimes they dance,
sometimes they bleed
from your fingers
onto the page.

Always, they wait
for you to notice
they are there,
because only you
can live your poems
into being
and write yourself
into seeing.

October Morning

I stepped into the woods
holding stories of my grandmothers
next to my heart.
The leaves were lit gold
from within and below
and two crows raised an alarm call.
After several timeless beats
of breath and silence
a deer lifted its white tail
and dashed away
leaving me to know it was my
own small form beneath the trees
who prompted the crows' warning.
The scent of cedar filled the air
as I crouched beneath
illuminated branches
on the stained glass glow
of brown oak
and yellow maple leaves.
Fragments of evergreen tips
scattered across the leaves,
small blue juniper berries
were bright against wet green moss,
while persimmons hung

peachy-rose beneath the sky,
watching me kneel there
caught between rays of sunlight
and enchantment.
A fallen tree carpeted with fungus
captivated me next,
the perfect spiraled whorls
gently cupping last night's raindrops.
I stepped down slabs of stone
under bowers of gold branches
and stopped beside a
wide hollow bowl
carved by rain, rock, and time.
"When I die,
you can leave me curled up here
and I'll be happy,"
I said to my husband,
for a moment clearly seeing
my own bones lying nestled
smoothed and ivory
across this bed of leaves and sunbeams.
He didn't answer,
but laid his hand across my hip
and together we scrambled

like mountain goats
past crimson mushrooms
up the steep slope
where oak leaves give way
to slick brown needles
and there we sat on the stones
smiling silently
and looking at the sunshine
through the pines.

For Mark Remer.

Blackberry Morning

The blackberry leaves
have deepened to burgundy
and I find
I love them in all seasons,
from the softly furred green curls
above the thorns in springtime,
to the white flowers daubed with
the rains of early summer,
to firm black berries in the heat
of a July sun,
to deep red leaves glowing
beneath a muted October sunrise,
to the still dusky red glinting
through beads of ice in winter.
Today three valiant roses lift
brave red petals
to the sky behind the canes
and a young deer steps nimbly
from behind the woodpile,
scuffing its hooves at me
in challenge,
as its black eyes meet mine.
Soft globes of persimmon
glimmer behind the crimson flags

of sumac and maple,
and yellow oak leaves scattered
across the gravel
form a path into autumn.
While I am endlessly enchanted
by the world of salt and sand
and wave,
I am also endlessly grateful
to live on land
where I can see the wheel
of the year turn before my eyes
and watch the cycles of life
unfold around me,
the story written by
blackberry,
breath,
and cloud.

Many Lands

I dreamed of crows
in the trees
black wings lifting
in the sun,
while I watched laughing
and feeling alive
with magic
in my veins.
Then three new birds came,
blue feathers and white necks,
bodies thin blades
against the grass,
necks and legs long
like herons.
I could see the sunlight
through the short and spiky
feathers at their throats
and suddenly I smelled
the sharp scent of decay
in the air,
while I wondered why
they had come to feed
in my forest of crowsong.
In the waking world,

a smooth brown deer
and her twin yearlings
lifted watchful heads,
ears swiveling
and white tails raised
as I passed them on the road,
maple leaves still scarlet and gold,
the frost curling the last roses
to black
and folding the mulberry leaves
into wilted umbrellas.
At home,
I dipped my hand
into my coat pocket
to find it
full of sand.
I let the grains
trail through my fingers
into the flowerbed
noticing I carry many lands
in my creases
and seams.

Message from Persimmon

Honor both the tart and tender.
Allow sweetness to develop.
and mellow with time.
Watch for signs and listen to seeds.
Let the touch of air be your guide.
When the right moment comes,
let go.

World Spirit

For a brief moment,
of inhale and exhale,
the whole world
felt new,
alight with possibility,
born again in this singular
fresh moment.
The rising sun in the east
under a blossoming bank
of gray clouds
somehow illuminating the
red, orange, and yellow leaves
in the west,
lit from below and within
with an ethereal glow.
Standing there
in this slender slice of quiet,
a stillpoint on
the ribbon of eternity
before the day rolls into life,
I could hear the World Spirit
breathing in the trees.

Perhaps

Perhaps today...
one full breath,
one soft gaze,
one moment of quiet
for your heart.

Where is your joy?

Dark Moon Night

The thing I most
want to remember
is how it feels to kneel on damp earth
palms spread against the leaves
calling my spirit back
from where it has wandered,
re-collecting the many tendrils
that have curled away,
scooping up the shards
that have scattered into realms
both digital and personal,
reweaving the threads of being
until I resettle my soul
whole
once more in my skin
on the dirt.
I will remember the muted
rainbow spirals of mushrooms
blossoming from a gray trunk
and the sound of coyotes rising
from the valley
on a dark moon night.

Samhain Magic

Listen.
I am the ancestor's song,
the deepening
of twilight into dusk,
the wild enchantment
of wolf song in the night
and owls on the wing.
I tell silent stories
in timeless whispers
that echo through bone
and blood.

In the tenderness of memory,
the blaze of inspiration,
the lantern's glow
through a dark and restless night,
I call you to
restoration,
renewal,
wholeness,
and hope.

First Frost (All Hallows Morning)

On all Hallows morning,
I stepped into a frozen world,
blackberry leaves
frosted burgundy
beneath a freezing sunrise.
A woodpecker trilled across the sky
swooping into the bare fingers
of the trees,
red crest bright against gray bark,
and five crows tumbled
black and sateen
over the rooftop
and away
while I stood shivering
beside the thorns
head tilted back and laughing
with the crows.
On the frozen road,
I kept stopping to take pictures
of frosty leaves,
glittering diamond bright and
entrancing in the early morning sun.
I was brought to my knees
by the sight of leaf imprints

pressed into the frozen
dirt of the road
perfect veins preserved,
the footsteps of fall
into winter.
I'll stop after this,
I said,
meaning that I would keep
walking properly and
stop discovering
this magic everywhere
and hearing poems in the air.
Oh, but I see the sunshine
on those truck tracks
through this golden field
of illuminated grasses
bending under a granulated
silver sheen.
At each moment something
sharp and wondrous appears:
cedar tips collected green
and aromatic on the stones,
a blanket of yellow mulberry
leaves fanned around a slender gray trunk,

bright scarlet berries
and oval green leaves on
a holly shrub,
a puffy junco bird
perched in the round
orange persimmons,
a small, rusty feather on
the asphalt
soft and real
beneath my fingertips.

May we never stop
seeing
the soft and real,
the sharp
and surprising,
the delight that carries us
across frozen stones.

Making Magic

I trust my own ability
to make magic,
to weave rituals
from bones
and memory,
to build ceremonies
of instinct and fingertips,
to trust the power
of intuition,
seed,
cypress,
and stone.

For Jenny Johnson.

Ragged Prayers

I swam up from
the velvet cloak
of sleep,
ragged prayers sliding
just beyond my reach,
fingers clutching empty space,
half-remembered words
gathered with tears
in the back
of my throat,
the questions breathing
under my skin,
when to open our hands
and let things slip away,
when to stretch
beyond the limits,
seizing the lost
and reknitting it whole,
sometimes, somehow,
doing both at the same time.
These tender threads
of fragile living,
these acts of sacramental
possibility.

Frosted Magic

I stood transfixed
at the end of the driveway
listening as frost laden leaves
took turns dropping
from the oak trees,
each one a distinct and
individual sound.
No wind,
just the drop and whirl
of each frozen piece
twirling to land on the road.
Three crows streaked black
and raucous against
the bright blue sky
and my feet began to move again.
Wonder of wonders,
today, imprints of fallen leaves
comprised entirely of frost
upon the road,
their dark sisters embedded
in a mosaic of light and shadow
while frost flowers
glitter in the field,
spiraled funnels curling out

from expanded stems.
I become fascinated
with a tiny world
I discover in the grass
made of patterned ice,
brown water,
and frosted seed heads.
It takes me minutes of marveling
before I recognize that
I am gazing, entranced,
into what is actually a rut
carved by a heavy tractor tire,
forming a miniature landscape
of crystalline beauty,
a tiny lake of frozen possibility
right beneath my numb
and wondering fingers,
my breath curling smoky
into the sunlight across a field
of frosty magic.

November

Ten years ago I bled
and bled some more,
soft globes dropping
from my clenched flesh
as I gripped a lavender
sachet in my hand
and let the pain enfold me
until the baby slipped
silent and small
into my gray pants.
I touched his face
with a careful finger
and was awed to see his
mouth drop gently open.
Two years before I'd dreamed
of a child that died
after three breaths,
I named him Noah and laid him
against my breast.
In this waking world
of blood and anguish
I name the tiny child in my hands
Noah too.
The blood continues
and all I can do

is sing to the goddess
as we take the long road
to the hospital.
No longer able to differentiate
between fainting or dying
I sing
so she, they, we, I
will know
that
for now
I am still alive.
The doctor leaves handprints
made of my blood on the bed
and her heartless words
across my soul.
My mother brings potato soup
from Panera
(I've never eaten theirs again)
and my father cleans the baby's body
with tender fingertips.
We lay him in an oval wooden box,
and my husband digs a hole
in stony, frozen ground
tears pouring
onto the shovel

and the cold, brown dirt.
We scatter rosemary and lavender
over the rocks
and say goodbye
to this third child
who never breathed.
Each November
under brown leaves
and gray rain,
I feel the death pangs again,
hear the knell of grief
tolling across somber hills,
and feel the longing in my bones
to retreat into the arms of sorrow,
to find a cave of keening
where I might let my body
curl into herself
remembering what it feels like
to hold despair and hope
clotted together in the space
of one finite
and weeping
womb.

For Noah.

Reminder

*Do only what you
have time to do.
Honor your limits.
Respect your
human-sized life.
Trust the unfolding.*

First Snow

The first snow has settled
and we walked past the marks
of hooves imprinted on the
fresh, white ground,
frozen leaves cupped forlornly
around the soft gray body
of a dead mole
in the path,
our steps careful on
ice-encased gravel
while crows streaked over
the frozen persimmons,
seed fluff glowing
on golden spires,
the blue air
sharp in our lungs.
The world is hushed
and holding,
time for sinking in,
enfolding.

Seen

To be seen is sacred,
when his hand
skims my back
or our eyes meet
over the heads
of our children
with a shared sigh.
To be embraced
in my messiness,
and anxiety,
my worry,
and tears,
my laugher,
and weariness,
held through it,
seen through it,
loved and
known through it.
To be seen is sacred
when the sky darkens to dusk,
when the rain clouds gather,
whether the sun rises
over the waves
or sets over the hills.

("to be seen" writing prompt from Jennifer Louden in The Oasis)

Lilith's Cold Moon Rising

May you become
a dangerous woman,
arms growing into wings
leathery and strong
stroking fearlessly across the night
into caverns where others
hesitate to tread.
May you let your howls rip
from your throat
under a pale moon,
the flames leaping up
to stroke your tongue
with passion and resolve,
the smoke curling around you
until you know not whether
you are flesh or fire.
Let the talons grow
from your fingers
and the juice of living
drip down your chin
as your feet move to the pulse
of an unseen drum.
Let your power rise into your blood
and ripple through your skin

like lightning.
Let your voice become thunder,
your tears become a flood,
your breath become wind
as you become
a force of nature,
elemental,
emergent,
and bold.
May you be incandescent
with purpose,
ferociously whole,
a world of fierce
and furious beauty
in your open hands.

Mess and Magic

This morning I tried
to work on my book
while the household debris
whirled around me.
The toilet has a ring of water
around it,
or is it pee,
the children come to report.
There's a weird smell in the kitchen.
I can't create like this,
I yell.
I want to be inspiring,
not so messy,
not like this.
I gesture frantically,
my hair wild,
my eyes frenzied.
I need to take a shower,
but I only have nine minutes
before it is time to leave
and I want to format
this title page.
I only want to make things
from a place

of beauty and peace,
I shout,
and then I take my shower
with my heart beating too fast
and my mind spinning with to-dos.
As we fly down the road
to homeschool co-op
(we will be late),
there is a big buck in the road.
It is hunting season and
I stop the car on the hill.
Our eyes meet for a moment,
he is still,
antlers wide,
shoulders broad and brown
in the early morning sun.
Run free, big guy,
I say,
run free.
If you go up the hill,
you will be at our house
and it is always a safe place.
This feels both true and beautiful.
Maybe beautiful things

don't only grow from peace,
maybe they grow from the
soil of living,
which holds both
blood and tears
muck and magic.

For the unnamed lost.

Trust

I trust the crows
in the field at dawn,
the watchful deer
alert
and cautious
behind tall brown grasses.
I trust the turn of
the seasons,
the bite creeping into the air,
the letting go of the vows
of youth,
the allowing that ripens
rose hips to red.
I trust the sound of the
red-shouldered hawk
at sunrise,
the tattered leaves
on my rosebush
that will somehow
be renewed once more,
the rusty beauty
of frost-bitten
blackberry bushes,
and my own

sharp,
persistent
flame.

Both/And

Just a soft reminder
that it is okay to be
Both/And:
Tart and tender.
Worn and wondrous.
Wild and weary.
Accepting of limits.
Refusing to surrender.
Grasping and gracious.
Scorched and shining.
Brilliantly ragged.
Raggedly brilliant.
You are broad enough
to contain the contradictions
and to love yourself through
them all.

For Stella Webb and the
Red Tent Circle.

November Afternoon

I watched a pileated woodpecker
busy in an oak tree
as I sat in the temple
busy with my thoughts.
Its red crested head
was bright against the gray bark
and brown leaves.
I opened the door to go into the woods
and startled two large deer
standing right by the temple porch.
They leaped away
and I was left standing there
whispering
it's okay, friends,
there's no need to run from me.
The crows call in the woods
and the poke plants have
frozen to brown,
spiky arms jutting
into the cool gray clouds
above the trees.

The Next Chapter

*May you allow the unfolding
to continue.
May you allow the mystery
to settle in.
May you allow the path
to be revealed.
May you allow yourself
to discover
what it feels like
to fully expand,
filling the corners
of your
very own life.*

Bargains

Everything has a cost,
sometimes it is high,
painful,
even brutal.
Sometimes it is the price you pay
for keeping some
shreds of your soul for yourself,
for reknitting wholeness
into your bones,
and refusing to cut yourself,
even if that is what is
being asked of you.
Sometimes costs are too high
and you need to turn away,
even though that may wound others.
Please know that keeping
your spirit intact
and tending to your heart
are good bargains.

Awareness

I wake with three things on my mind:
The sound of red grass beneath my feet.
The sound of crows on the wing.
The sound of questions in the air.
We walk and there are four things
on my mind:
Mist hanging across gray hills
and sending smoky wisps into
fallow fields.
A leaf coasting all the way from treeline
to the road as if piloted by a tiny warrior
windsurfing through the fall.
The surprising bright orange flare
of bittersweet
leaning over a worn fence.
Wild turkeys spreading wide wings
and coasting away by the pond
while a calm deer and her black-eyed baby
watch warily from the field.
I see nine crows creasing the misty morning
beneath a canopy of gray.
I hear the sound of brown gravel
beneath my shoes
as I follow the path back home.

Dreams

I surfaced from waves of sleep
with a message from dawn
clutched in my hand,
but when I unclenched my fist
to reveal my insight
it glided away from my needy fingers
onto the noisy black wings
of a crow
who bore it away
across the hills
and left me wondering
what it was I thought
I knew.

Sunlit Rye

I walked at 2:30 on a brown road
after the rain
having again expected
both the hours
and me
to hold more than is possible.
We need to go back inside,
but for a moment
nothing else matters
because I see a leaf with sun on it.
There is a soft patch of moss across the stone,
the light behind the leaf
gives the impression of a flame
against the gray rocks,
and a shaft of wild rye
holds sunlight
with an easy grace
I could learn from.
Three crows have gathered in the tree tops
black wings catching the afternoon
and in the tall branches of a cedar
I find a whisper of forgiveness.
At home again, sitting in the wind
with the taste of

tears mingling with chamomile tea
upon my tongue,
and a pale crescent moon peeking through
the clouds,
words from unmet friends
soften the tension around my thoughts
and brush my tight shoulders
with a breath of love
and witnessing.
I hear the breeze murmuring
in the leaves,
trickling quietly down
the cedar boughs
and coming to rest across my fingers:
there is so much that crowds around you that
is unnecessary,
can you exhale and let it drift away
with these pink-kissed clouds
and sunlit wild rye?

For Barbara Holt and the Creative Spirit
Circle.

Aging Well

I hope aging well
means you have splendid orgasms,
that you choose the best chocolate,
and eat plenty of it.
I hope it means keeping dates
with sunrises and sunsets,
with reading whatever you want
and sleeping when you need to.
I hope aging well means
resting well
and seeing everything you desire.
I hope it means great mugs
of exotic teas
and many tastes of adventure.
I hope aging well means
creating beauty,
loving boldly,
and watching wisely.
I hope it means
speaking your truth
when needed and
keeping silence when sensible.
I hope aging well
has nothing to do

with your hair color,
your weight,
your eyesight,
or your skin,
and everything to do
with the colors of your
wild inspiration,
the depth of your inspired living,
the width of your passion,
and your powerful,
potent
loving
of this life.

River Night

Late this afternoon
we walked at the river
for the first time in far
too many days.
We watched gray clouds
roll across the sky
as the last thin slices of pink
dropped behind the trees.
We looked for beaver
by peeled blond saplings
and watched an armadillo
rustling through the tall grasses
on the bank.
We leaned over the small spring
and witnessed the newborn
yet eternal water bubble up
and spread past shocks of
green watercress.
We gazed at a watchful brown deer
for long moments—
us on the small cliff
overlooking the confluence
and it below on the rocks
at the river's edge,

until suddenly two companions joined it
and they all flashed their white tails and
ran off through the water,
splashing and clattering
against the stones.
The bats began to dip and dive
low over the water
and we circled the field,
smelling the river
and watching
the mysteries
of an evening unfold.

Forgetting and Remembering

I am always forgetting
and remembering
how it feels to take a break,
to need one
and to step away.
To lie on the floor
when my body and my heart
cry out for stillness and peace.
How to reach out my hand
to my own tattered self
when I am starving for my own company,
ravenous for the space
inside my own head
where wholeness dwells.
I am always forgetting
and remembering
how to pay exquisite attention
to the soft dark leaves
and how they form prints upon
the sand of the roadway.
I am always forgetting
and remembering
how the soft
kiss of the wind

can restore my soul,
how magic dwells
in shafts of sunlight
tiny mosses,
and moon shadows
on brown rocks.
I am always forgetting
that I can't ever get
it all figured out
and remembering that
I don't have to.

Forgetting and Remembering prompt from
the Oasis from Jennifer Louden.

Curious

I was just getting the mail,
but wispy white clouds
cast feathered
threads across an ocean
of blue sky
and a gray moon watched over
a flock of robins
clustered together
in a cedar tree.
The late afternoon sunlight
shining through dried asters,
starlike bursts of crisped gray
Queen Anne's lace,
and ethereally glowing bluestem,
called my spirit to join them.
Kneeling there on a tussock
of tight dry grasses,
the ground beneath my knees
felt warm
almost as if a small dog
lay curled against my folded legs.
As I sat transfixed,
crouched and staring out of
golden seedheads

like a wild thing,
small, alert, sunwarmed,
and part of the curious,
I found myself thinking:
isn't this the real task of living,
to remember how to
take care of ourselves,
breathing slow
and tending to
those things
that are invisible
to the incurious.

What You Love

*Please let what you love
bubble to the surface
of your life,
even if it feels like
there isn't time.
It matters.
You matter.
What you love
is part of the fuel
of the universe.
It belongs in this world
and it can only move
through you.*

Holding Our Souls Together

Walking in the morning
our steps steady on brown gravel,
a surprising variety of cars pass us
and Mark says:
"I wonder if people see us
and think this is all we ever do,
walk on the road."
I say, fervently, "if they do, I would say: don't
you know, this is how
we hold our souls together!"
and I lift my arm, my small, indefatigable fist
of resistance,
to show how serious I am
about which I speak.
There is no exaggeration here,
that crow crossing the road
and coasting into silent trees
carries life itself on its wings.
Those frost flowers tight curled
and opening into ribbons of
delicacy,
they are both ephemeral
and world-sustaining.
That hawk, perched solemnly

in the treetop,
the same shape as a small penguin
as it studies the field,
is an encounter with divine curiosity.
The branches that bend over the roadway,
with a tiny bird's nest gripped impossibly in
the wind
held aloft even in the bony fingers
of winter,
is a lesson in hope
and determination.
Those hoof prints on frozen ground
by the mailbox,
those soft black eyes in the brambles,
this is communion
with the sacramental business
of being whole,
fed to the marrow with the real magic
of breathing in the wild enchantment
of here.
I must have time to see,
to move,
to watch the sun
and the clouds,

to feel the wind,
and my heart beat in my wrist,
to know that I am alive,
and so too,
am wondrous with possibility.

For Mark Remer.

A Coincidence of Magic

Through the magic of coincidence
or the coincidence of magic
I made a decision about the
remainder of the decade
based on the flight of a single
black crow on a gray horizon
and a soft brown fawn
with a calm black gaze,
munching green ears of mullein
by the burgundy blackberry brambles,
who reminded me I can coax
a temporary pause
from an overfull life.
It is not a permanent surrender
to lay some things aside
and to take up watching
the ordinary amazement
of a normal day unfold.
We all have to make choices,
perhaps sometimes these may
be guided by crows and fawns
instead of logic and rationality,
and may they lead us into
startling beauty,

surprising truth,
and the life-changing,
world transforming power,
of mundane wonder.

Message from the Solstice Crone

Listen.
I invite you into cave time,
be still and listen,
watch, and know.
There is a time for rest,
renewal,
and silent,
witnessing peace.
Steep in your wisdom.
Stir up your spirit.
Savor your flavor.
I am twilight and shadow.
Deepen with me
and become
the container
of your own emergence.

Solstice Night

And so the sun sets
on the longest night.
May you descend into a time
of deep rest
and nourish your dreams.
May you coax the ember
of your hope into life
and nestle it close to your heart
nurtured by your soft breath
and your wise secrets.
Breathe deep and be,
breathe deep and see,
breathe deep
in peace.
Let yourself pause
in the sacred wonder
of cave time,
the rich darkness
in which all things
become possible.

Longing

What are you withholding
from yourself?
What longing are you
letting languish?
What desire are you
denying?
What are you ignoring
that you crave
and need to thrive?
What is your heart whispering,
your soul crying out for,
your body pulsing to uncover
and allow?
What do you see if you
dare to look
into your own
cupped hands?

Questions

Is there magic even here?
I queried on a dreary morning.
Swiftly, the answer
arrived
gliding in on silent wings:
Yes, great glittering strands of it
laced through
All
Things
waiting for you to see it,
or not,
it is up to you.

Ragged Prayers

May you hold on to
tattered hopes
and slender dreams,
cracked promises
and broken fears.
May you hold on to
ragged prayers
and frayed patience,
shredded peace,
and scattered power.
May you coax new worlds from
the worn embers
you've kept alive with
only your breath
tears and blood,
then open your hands
and let the rest of the ashes
drift away on the wind.
May you gather the scraps
of your forlorn and weary days
and may you weave new stories
from the shreds of your patience
and the shards of your prayers.

The Heart of Wonder

The day dawned peach and lavender
against snow-covered trees
and we stepped away into a landscape
of frozen delight.
The whole world feels
hushed and holding,
still and white,
shimmering with possibility.
Gleefully, we become amateur trackers
in this soft white wonderland,
the road yet untouched by tires.
We follow the soft paw prints of a bobcat
leading from the deep woods
out onto the road
padding along until they intersect
with the double-hoof-print draaaag
of Limpy and her baby,
the mother deer with one lame leg
that we have watched and rooted for
over the last two years.
There is a meeting point between the tracks,
the deer continuing one direction
and the bobcat another.
Then, the small scurry marks

of a mouse running from the
seed-rich stand of wild grasses
in the center of the crossroads
across to the other side
where they form a circle of tracks
around a twiggy sapling.
A set of broadly spaced tracks
now appear, long brush marks in the snow,
one in the center of the circle,
the second outside it
and the mouse tracks cease.
We surmise an owl has left
these brushy marks across the snow.
We feel like detectives,
like scientists,
like explorers
and are giddy with excitement
in this glittering world.
We slip away beneath the trees
to the secret pines overlooking
a silent gully formed of stone and time
and stand together by lichen laden
boulders beside the trunks
of tall and ancient pines,

each hatched square of bark
topped with a perfect cap of snow.
The sun illuminates one side of the hill
and the other is shadowy and cold.
We know, suddenly, that we are
perhaps the first humans to leave footprints
in the snow at this
point of pine and stone
in countless years
and the moment feels small and sacred
invisible and yet significant
on the ribbon of time.
We lean into one another's shoulders;
there are no re-dos of this day,
I say,
we only see it or we don't,
the moment doesn't come back.
And, we are grateful, so grateful
and humbled
to have chanced to look
into the heart of wonder
on a snowy and shining morning
in an everyday world.

A Blessing for Your Whole Self

May you tend your heart
with the careful fingers of
exposed truth.
May you guard your soul
with the fine threads
of secret wisdom.
May you soothe your soft body
with the liniment of time
and delight.
May you nurture your hearth
with a rich stew
of both solitude and community,
laughter and reflection,
brewing up a cup of wonder
for each who cares to drink.
May you excavate your peace
from the rubble of
compulsive pleasing
and let it rest on your fingers
like a bluebird on a sunsoaked tree.
May you find your power
right beside you,
not lost,
just waiting to be picked up

with loving hands
and stretched gently back
across your bones.

*Let your
wild prayers
teach you
where it all
lives.*

Come Join the Circle!

Membership in the Creative Spirit Circle FREE and packed with beautiful, bountiful resources, including:

- A free Womanrunes e-course.
- Companion online classrooms.
- Goddess Studies and Ritual course.
- Virtual circle opportunities in our Facebook group.
- Resources for Red Tents, sacred ceremonies, and rituals.
- Prayer cards, oracle card layouts, and mandalas.
- Access to Divine Imperfections sculptures.
- Monthly *Creative Spirit Circle Journal* with resources such as ceremony outlines, articles, book recommendations, sneak peeks, and special freebies.

**Claim your place in the Circle:
brigidsgrove.com/come-join-the-circle**

Connect with Brigid's Grove

- brigidsgrove.com
- patreon.com/brigidsgrove
- facebook.com/brigidsgrove
- instagram.com/brigidsgrove
- brigidsgrove.etsy.com
- Creative Spirit Circle Facebook Group: facebook.com/groups/ brigidsgrovecreativespiritcircle

About the Author

Molly has been gathering the women to circle, sing, celebrate, and share since 2008. She plans and facilitates women's circles, Red Tents, seasonal retreats and rituals, Pink Tent mother-daughter circles, and family ceremonies in 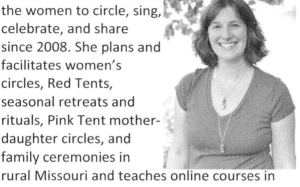 rural Missouri and teaches online courses in Red Tent facilitation and Practical Priestessing.

Molly is a priestess who holds MSW, M.Div, and D.Min degrees and wrote her dissertation about contemporary priestessing in the U.S.

Molly is the author of *Womanrunes, Earthprayer, She Lives Her Poems,* the *Goddess Devotional,* and *The Red Tent Resource Kit*. She writes about women's circles, nature, practical priestessing, creativity, family ritual, and the goddess at Brigid's Grove, SageWoman Magazine, and Feminism and Religion.

About Brigid's Grove

Molly and Mark co-create original Story Goddesses, goddess sculptures, mini goddess pendants, and ceremony kits at brigidsgrove.com (and etsy!). They publish *Womanrunes* books and decks, based on the work of Shekhinah Mountainwater.

Brigid's Grove integrates Molly's priestess work and goddess studies with our family's shared interests in ceremony, art, gemstones, metalwork, nature, and intentional, creative living.

Brigid is the Irish triple goddess of smithcraft, poetry, and midwifery. She is also a Christian saint associated with midwives, birthing mothers, and infants.